THE UNICORN PROBLEM

MITCHELL J. FRANGADAKIS

The Unicorn Problem
Copyright 2016 Mitchell J. Frangadakis
All Rights Reserved

First Wisdom Artists Edition 2016

Cover and Formatting by Formatting by R.A. Mizer of ShoutLines.
For more information visit Shoutlinesdesign.com.

To reproduce or use any of the information contained in this book, please contact wisdom@mind.net.

Published in the United States of America

PRAISE FOR THE UNICORN PROBLEM

"The Unicorn Problem astonishes with its capacity to rationally examine the underbelly of reason, deftly shedding our deeply held assumptions on what it means to know anything at all."

Sarah Marshank, author of Being Self-ish

"This book is a treasure, not jut another volume for your coffee table. Frangadakis is speaking not just theoretically, but from actual realization of the meditative states that he is clarifying in his book, The Unicorn Problem. The Buddhist path begins with correct understanding. This is a priceless addition to that first step."

Junpo Denis Kelly, 83rd Patriarch, Rinzai Tradition/Zen, Hollow Bones Zen

---

'Unicorn' is a masterful survey of the human race's collective philosophical brilliance, featuring course after course of immensely rewarding, creatively integrated philosophical insights. If you are looking for something that will inspire and equip you (or anyone) to undertake further individual inquiry into the nature and practice of living a good life, you need look no further."

Paul Richards/ Founder and Director, Sente Center

For my wife, my dearest love and best friend.

"CALL IT A SIN TO LET SLIP A TRUTH."

Robert Browning (1812-1889)

"And are we to suppose, I said, that the philosopher sets any value on other pleasures in comparison with the pleasure of knowing the truth, and in that pursuit abiding, ever learning, not so far indeed from the heaven of pleasure? Does he not call the other pleasures necessary, under the idea that if there were no necessity for them, he would rather not have them?"

Plato (427-347 BCE)

"What is honorable, what is fair, what is becoming, what is noble, what is generous, takes possession of the heart, and animates us to embrace and maintain it. What is intelligible, what is evident, what is probable, what is true, procures only the cool assent of the understanding; and gratifying a speculative curiosity, puts an end to our researches."

David Hume (1711-1776)

TABLE OF CONTENTS

Prologue	....	1
Author's Note	....	3
Introduction	....	5
Chapter 1 Understanding the Problem	....	11
Chapter 2 What Should We Believe?	....	29
Chapter 3 In Pursuit of the Truth	....	47
Chapter 4 The Hard Problem	....	67
Chapter 5 Faith and Reality	....	95
Chapter 6 Logic and other Presuppositions	....	115
Chapter 7 From Illusion to Truth	....	137
Chapter 8 Is nothing sacred?	....	161
Chapter 9 Embracing Doubt	....	189
Epilogue The Moral of the Story?	....	205
Afterword	....	217
Acknowledgments	....	227

PROLOGUE

Although the written language of ancient Greece was both comprehensive and sophisticated, Socrates believed that writing and reading were ineffective and inefficient communication skills. Words lying on a page were not capable of clarifying or defending the author's position and, he believed, would undoubtedly create misunderstandings in the mind of the reader. For Socrates, the written word was "dead," and only through the spoken word – the dialectic – would we arrive at the truth about any topic of interest, especially the topic of Truth itself. Verbal discourse, he believed, was the only way to be fully understood. He also concluded that having such ready access to information in books would diminish one's ability to recall from memory and consequently inhibit the ability to reason. And though I might agree that there is some truth to his claims, my own concern is that I make clear my purpose in adding to those volumes of information.

Various religious doctrines are mentioned throughout this text, but I should stress that I am not a religious scholar, nor is this a book on comparative religion. My personal religious experiences have to do with my early upbringing in the Christian Greek Orthodox Church and my later involvement in Buddhism. As a consequence, I refer to those two religious doctrines most often within this text. In general, I employ Christianity to represent our Western monotheistic traditions and Buddhism as the primary representative of Eastern religious doctrines, which is not to suggest that all Eastern religions or philosophical systems are necessarily in agreement with Buddhist perspectives. I have always been intrigued by the epistemological claims contained within religious doctrines, East and West alike, and how these propositions compare with the truth-bearing claims of

THE UNICORN PROBLEM

philosophy and contemporary science. And though there are countless books out there in the categories of science, philosophy, and religion that are no doubt more insightful and informative than anything I might be able to offer, I felt compelled to add this book in order to address and underscore what I am whimsically referring to as the Unicorn Problem. From antiquity to this day, this central epistemological issue has provoked not only a war of words, but actual holy wars and executions in the name of Truth. To date, there are no clear victors and paradoxically, no clear losers.

The Unicorn Problem is this: What should we believe as true? And who or what should we trust in validation of that truth? Furthermore, how can we determine what is both true and certain, and concomitantly, what is necessarily false? What constitutes a truth-bearing claim that we may accept without reservation? This dilemma lies at the root of all knowledge systems or claims about truth that I or anyone else might make, be they religious, mystical, scientific, or philosophical. Just that fact alone makes it a critical problem worth a second look by anyone who is interested in living a contemplative life of conscious self-reflection, a life of personal integrity, a life described by Plato as the "examined life."

This book is not intended as a definitive guide as to what constitutes ultimate Truth. Rather, its purpose is to encourage further inquiry and appraisal of what it is in your own beliefs and in your own spiritual life that may require further review. Today's Internet can provide us with access to volumes of information on almost any subject matter, including the most current information from modern science and theoretical physics explaining the highly impersonal origins of our physical world. And yet, the essential questions concerning the human condition and the ultimate purpose of our individual lives remains for each of us to solve. In my view this requires a critical self-examination of the entrenched beliefs and assumptions that determine how we live our lives and, perhaps most importantly, define our moral outlook.

AUTHOR'S NOTE

A brief comment about the *thought experiments* you will find at the beginning of most chapters: I have found that my students – and most people – either love or hate them. I happen to love them *(See addendum at the end of this section)*. There is general agreement that thought experiments are not intended to solve the problems they pose with concrete answers; they are instead provocations guiding us into deeper and subtler thinking about the various narratives presented. Thought experiments are usually of three types: critical, explanatory, and apologetic. In this wise, "critical" means that the thought exercise is designed to refute or question some previously accepted proposition. The experiment proposed by Anthony Flew about the Cosmic Gardener at the beginning of Chapter III, *In Pursuit of Truth*, is an example of this kind. Scientists tend to prefer Explanatory thought experiments. An example of this type is Isaac Newton's (1642-1726) thought experiment regarding the motion of the moon around the earth; this is at the beginning of Chapter VIII, *Is Nothing Sacred?* Apologetic thought experiments oftentimes defend some moral or ontological principle, and I will let the reader discover those independently.

ADDENDUM

"There is widespread agreement that thought experiments play a central role both in philosophy and in the natural sciences and general acceptance of the importance and enormous influence and value of some of the well-known thought experiments in the natural sciences, like Maxwell's demon, Einstein's elevator or Schrödinger's cat. The 17th century saw some of its most brilliant practitioners in Galileo, Descartes, Newton, and Leibniz. And in our own time, the creation of quantum mechanics and relativity are almost unthinkable without the crucial role played by thought experiments. Much of ethics, philosophy of language, and philosophy of mind is based firmly on the results of thought experiments as well, including Searle's Chinese room or Putnam's twin earth. Philosophy, even more than the sciences, would be severely impoverished without thought experiments, which suggests that a unified theory of thought

THE UNICORN PROBLEM

experiments is desirable to account for them in both the sciences and the humanities." – *Stanford Encyclopedia of Philosophy (S.E.P.)*

INTRODUCTION

"I believe in everything until it's disproved. So I believe in fairies, the myths, and dragons. It all exists, even if it's in your mind. Who's to say that dreams and nightmares aren't as real as the here and now?"
John Lennon (1940-1980)

"Do fairies live in the multiverse?"
Astrophysicist Marcelo Gleiser (1959-)

Unicorn: "A fabulous beast, usually having the head and body of a horse, the hind legs of an antelope, the tail of a lion, sometimes the beard of a goat, and as its chief feature a long, sharp, twisted horn set in the middle of its forehead...The earliest description is that of Ctesias, who states that there were in India white wild asses celebrated for their fleetness of foot, having on the forehead a horn a cubit and a half in length, colored white, red and black; from the horn were made drinking cups which were a preventative of poisoning."
Encyclopedia Britannica

***

When I first began teaching the Philosophy of Religion course at Southern Oregon University, I asked my friend, colleague and Chair of our philosophy program, Prakash Chenjeri, why we didn't teach Eastern religions as part of the curriculum. After all, not everyone is a Jew, Christian, or Muslim. Why not include Hinduism, Buddhism, Jainism, even African and other religious alternatives to our monotheistic view of human creation and purpose? Wasn't it

THE UNICORN PROBLEM

important, I asked, for our students to be exposed to the religious doctrines of India and the ancient Vedas, for example?

I asked this because, although I was raised in the Greek Orthodox tradition, I have adopted Buddhist practices over the last 45 years of my life. I felt qualified to teach my students something about Buddhist views, even if only at the most rudimentary level. So why, I wondered, offer only Western religions in a Philosophy of Religion course? In fact, I had noticed that many of the current books written by philosophers on religion now included a strong dose of the Eastern religious and philosophical traditions, most especially Buddhist doctrine.

His response to my question was simple and direct: Westerners should understand their own traditions first, despite the fact that religious and philosophical speculations on both sides of the divide do share a common ground. In order to better understand ourselves in today's world we should understand our own Western conceptual underpinnings – the original ideas and theories that were developed from our ancient religious and philosophical traditions, culminating in our current scientific understanding of the world and our place in it.

Although we have recently added a course in East Indian philosophy for our upper division students, I realized that there might be additional reasons why teaching only Western religions through the philosophical lens could be readily justified as a stand-alone course. Perhaps most importantly, I no longer believe that the religious traditions of the East and West are so different from one another. I am aware of the significant doctrinal difference, but the overall intentions, goals, and moral practices of all the major religions remain quite similar if not the same. In addition, I have come to the realization over the years that philosophy is not simply a subject to be studied, at least not in the formal sense that we think of studying biology or anthropology or any other subject. It is more a *process to be enacted*, an attitude and orientation of the mind and heart to be adopted and put into practice – what I like to call a *radical attitude adjustment*. I would also propose that this philosophical attitude is essentially skeptical, which means orienting our minds towards a deep inquiry into the human condition and critically examining the ideas to which we are most attached. Philosophy keeps our minds present and accounted for by constantly questioning our fixed views and beliefs, allowing us in the end to draw our own distinctions and conclusions about Truth and Reality. This cognitive shift in attitude transforms even the most mundane and normal activities of our lives, and so becomes a life-long endeavor to truly understand the judgments we make and the actions we take.

Let us propose philosophy as a method for the elimination of confusion and the enhancement of clarity in the understanding of our world; it is an internal, cognitive discipline that each of us must consciously embrace and develop if we are to actualize our potential to live a happy and fulfilled life. Developing these attributes enhances the quality of our interactions in the world and ultimately becomes part of a collective process, much as the science of today is the product of a collective enterprise. I would argue that philosophy provides a blueprint from which to work, a purchase when contemplating any system of knowledge, including any and all religious doctrines, and acts as a common denominator across all intellectual and aesthetic fields of study.

I also think that philosophy, much like all religious inquiries, stands as testimony to our innate human curiosity...that impulse to incessantly look toward the stars and explore the depths of our own minds seeking understanding and a lasting clarity. We could, for example, thumb through countless volumes in our need for Truth within the philosophy of religion (both Eastern and Western traditions), or into history, science, literature, and so on, addressing each discipline through the same philosophical orientation, necessarily grounded in conceptual and diagnostic rigor. Chenjeri is fond of saying that philosophy is the process of unpacking concepts, regardless of their origin, be they from our Western religious traditions or otherwise. I also appreciate the description of philosophy from philosopher Michael Sandel: the process of *making*

THE UNICORN PROBLEM

the familiar strange, a sentiment that can be traced back to the origins of philosophy itself.

Let's also recall that in Plato's dialogs, his friend and philosophical mentor Socrates would ask questions for which even he had no sufficient answers. The Oracle at Delphi had proclaimed Socrates the wisest man in Athens, but only because he was that rare individual who realized how little he really knew. This is a truism that is demonstrated every day by all those who sincerely inquire into any body of knowledge – be it the arts, music, literature, religion, science or philosophy. They eventually discover precisely what the Oracle meant. In this regard, there is a quote from the philosopher and mathematician Bertrand Russell (1872-1970) that has remained with me over the years: "We must learn how to live with uncertainty without being frozen by doubt." Yet, if we accept the infallibility of the Oracle at Delphi, despite Socrates's life-long mission to prove otherwise, we are left with a "unicorn" of sorts, a logical difficulty that seems unresolvable: If Socrates knows that he doesn't know, isn't that a form of knowledge? Or perhaps the wisdom of Socrates is not knowledge at all: it is simply a belief that Socrates holds to be sacrosanct.

As the futurist Buckminster Fuller (1896-1983) once sagely remarked, our planet did not come with an instruction manual, and this home of ours, mysterious organism that it is, appears desperately in need of one. Unfortunately, we have to develop our earth-manual day by day in the hope that we survive long enough to figure out who we are, where we are, and how we got here. As if this task isn't daunting enough, every individual human being must wrestle with his or her own psyche—that privileged access that each of us has into our solitary soul—and understand for him or herself if there be a purpose to fulfill and a moral law to follow in this brief span we call a human lifetime. All of this can be very disorienting, and we might justifiably ask: Is it possible for any human being to know what is absolutely certain and real? Can human beings know Truth?

As Bertrand Russell (1872-1970) goes on to say in in his book, *Problems of Philosophy*: "The value of philosophy is, in fact, to be sought largely in its very uncertainty. The man who has no tincture of philosophy goes through life imprisoned in the prejudices derived from common sense, from the habitual beliefs of his age or his nation, and from convictions, which have grown up in his mind without the co-operation or consent of his deliberate reason. To such a man the world tends to become definite, finite, obvious; common objects rouse no questions, and unfamiliar possibilities are contemptuously rejected."

The constant refrain in regard to all claims about what is certain and what is not – including *all* religious claims – is this: *How do we know?* How is any judgment deemed to be completely true or false? Even if I claim that an absolute or infallible Truth lies beyond language and conceptual understanding itself, as it appears to be in religious experiences or epiphanies, isn't it still fair to ask why this claim of Truth should be accepted? What is proof enough and where might the certainty we seek be secured?

Every system of knowledge must struggle with the problem of *justifying* any claims made about Truth and Reality. After all, if we operate within belief systems alone, with no criteria to serve as verification for those beliefs, then any claim about truth will do. The vital element in any religious, philosophical, or scientific doctrine – the cornerstone, if you will – is knowledge itself, and how it is that we claim to possess it. The constant uncertainty that everyone must contend with – no matter what walk of life, no matter what his or her philosophical or religious preferences might be – is what I am referring to here as the Unicorn Problem.

Princeton philosopher Thomas Nagel (1937-) pinpoints it best when he writes: "…We step back to find that the whole system of justification and criticism, which controls our choices and supports our claims to rationality, rests on responses and habits that we never question, that we should not know how to defend without circularity, and to which we shall continue to adhere even after they are called into question."

CHAPTER 1
UNDERSTANDING THE PROBLEM

"There is some danger in pointing out the obvious."
G. Santayana (1863-1952)

"Nan-in, a Japanese master during the Meiji era (1868-1912), received a university professor who came to inquire about Zen. Nan-in served tea. He poured his visitor's cup full, and then kept on pouring. The professor watched the overflow until he no longer could restrain himself. "It is overfull. No more will go in!"
"Like this cup," Nan-in said, "you are full of your own opinions and speculations. How can I show you Zen unless you first empty your cup?"
Zen Story

WHAT UNICORNS?

We are, as former U.S. Secretary of Defense Donald Rumsfeld put it so succinctly, perpetually surrounded by "unknown unknowns," and as such, we cannot grasp the magnitude of what we don't even know we don't know. We live inside a mystery we call Life. We think we know physical stuff, but no one has yet touched the ground of matter, despite the fact that we have been through many phases where we believe we have. We think we can grasp the nature of the mind, but our ideas and emotions never corral its essence or the complexity of its tapestry. And just the simple fact of human awareness is enigmatic by its very nature. Nonetheless, we tether ourselves to beliefs and opinions about the world and our place in it,

THE UNICORN PROBLEM

but those convictions can never be publicly justified to the point beyond all doubt. We may feel assured that our convictions regarding life are true, but self-assurance is often far removed from reality.

In the history of Western theology and natural philosophy there has remained a long-standing search for absolute knowledge, a type of knowledge about which it would be impossible to be wrong. I believe a strong argument could be made that demonstrates how this quest is more a psychological need of humanity in general – our biological inheritance as a species – than an actual theological or intellectual possibility. We may have to admit, especially those of us who feel the need for conceptual clarity in our lives, that our search for certainty is like a human appetite or desire, a process that satiates at somewhat predictable thresholds but quickly grows dissatisfied as our minds begin to grumble once again. This kind of certainty is both provisional and temporary, and doesn't approach this ancient standard for Truth.

It remains that all of our conceptual endeavors – be they religious, scientific or otherwise – bear endemic difficulties that seem insurmountable, and they are the very difficulties that comprise the Unicorn Problem. For example, we cannot conceptually resolve the fundamental epistemological problem of an *infinite regress*. It remains impossible for us to supply sufficient evidence for our truth-bearing claims, which is to say that we cannot know absolutely that those claims are true.

What we *can* do is understand why Aristotle took a strong position regarding the infinite regress problem, insisting that we must pick a starting point – some self-evident truth or truths – in order to speak of knowledge at all. Without at least a few simple categories that point in one direction or another (a simple definition or two will do), we can't even begin a conversation about Truth, Justice, Reality and so on. If we claim that we possess knowledge of any kind, then don't we have some responsibility to provide an account of our position, doing our best to explain why we believe it? Doesn't any truth-bearing claim, regardless of its source, demand justification, and doesn't any system of justification rest upon assumptions that are more often than not, accepted without question?

If we then announce that no claim is to be accepted as true unless it can be satisfactorily justified, what justifies this position? Common sense? Reason? Intuition? To which starting point should we regress? It appears that even adopting the position that any truth-bearing claim requires justification cannot itself be readily justified. This is the type of conceptual knot that self-referencing arguments inevitably create. For example, when Socrates refuted the Sophists position that "man is the measure of all things," he asked if this claim was relatively or absolutely true. If the Sophists' final position about truth was simply relative, then their convictions held no more validity than countless other claims about truth. If on the other hand, *all* truth-bearing claims are indeed relative, then the Sophists were refuting themselves by insisting their position was absolute. How should this knot be cut? By ignoring logical contradictions?

For Socrates, the end of the epistemological journey – or at least a resting place – was *aporia*, which literally means "without passage". Some scholars have argued that the whole point of the Socratic dialectic and its method (*elenchus*) is to reach this conceptual impasse. When Socrates asked a famous general to define courage, the general realized soon enough that he could not answer the question and retreated in a huff. When the gadfly of Athens asked an artist to tell him what is meant by beauty, all the artist could offer were examples of beauty, but as for beauty itself, he could not say. The Socratic dialectic often left the most loquacious and confident conversationalists both speechless and angry. Plato characterized this process as a form of cognitive shock, analogous to the torpedo fish that stuns its unsuspecting prey.

As for the ultimate goal of this painful process, Plato (through the character of Socrates) put it this way: "...when a person starts on the discovery of the absolute by the light of reason only, and without any assistance of sense, and perseveres until by pure intelligence he arrives at the perception of the absolute good, he at last finds

THE UNICORN PROBLEM

himself at the end of the intellectual world, as in the case of sight at the end of the visible." —*Plato's Republic*

In order to comprehend why Socrates would have this objective in mind, constantly leading conversations into conceptual dead-ends and leaving his conversation partner unnerved, we must remember that his entire claim to wisdom was predicated on the conscious knowledge of his own ignorance. In exposing the inherent contradictions in his interlocutor's claims, *aporia* was revealed, and paradoxically wisdom was thereby magnified. Borrowing from Oscar Wilde, we might say that in pointing out these contradictions, Socrates was forcing truth to stand on its head in order to draw attention to itself. I might add that this "end of the intellectual world" is the same goal sought in the Zen koan system with its inherent paradoxes, hence my conclusion that Socrates was wise in the same sense that a Zen master is deemed wise.

This ancient Greek notion of *aporia* may in fact be the best description of the Unicorn Problem. If we consider conceptual issues wherein two claims are equally possible when considered separately, yet when taken together nullify one another, then we are definitely assessing a wild Unicorn.

The simple act of observing a stick submerged in water, offered by the philosopher Nicholas Rescher (1928-), is an example of what I mean:

    1) What the sight of our eyes tells us is to be believed.

    2) Sight tells us the stick is bent.

    3) What the touch of our hand tells us is to be believed.

    4) Touch tells us the stick is straight.

Which of the two sense fields should determine what is truly real: sight or touch? We might argue that the stick *appears* bent when in water but *really* is not. We know this through the application of reason in understanding and explaining light refraction and the illusions it can create. Yet the application of reason imposes its own complications. The ancient philosopher, Zeno (5th c. B.C.E.), offered logical demonstrations that purportedly proved that *all* motion is an illusion. The arrow flying through the air cannot possibly move – logically speaking. As to the problem of the bent stick, we must ask ourselves how much more reliable is touch when compared with sight, the very same sense that assures us that the sun circles the earth? It seems all our sense fields are filled with their own array of perceptual tricks and misdirection. Ultimately, it appears that we must choose between our sense fields and pure logic, wondering which to trust as the basis of our knowledge. Thus, most of us have no problem accepting the logic of the earth's motion around the sun, despite the contrary conclusion that our faculty of vision demands of us.

As another example of sensory misdirection, how do we explain the incongruity between what we sense and the actual fact that our earth is spinning on its axis at a thousand miles an hour while simultaneously hurtling through space at approximately 77,000 miles per hour? Add to this that our entire solar system is also racing through space towards the constellation Hercules at approximately 446,000 miles per hour. Amazingly, we feel none of this. Once again, the question becomes: should we trust our sensations or trust logic? Human beings are only capable of sensing the tiniest portion of the electro-magnetic field, such that we can't hear the high frequencies that dogs hear and can't see the ultra-violet light that honeybees see. All of our sense fields have normal thresholds that limit our perceptual abilities. Even our most fundamental feelings of pleasure and pain (upon which the Hedonist moral view is predicated) can play tricks on us. The Russian physiologist Ivan Pavlov (1849-1936) found in his research that at a certain threshold of intense pain, the subjective feeling reverses to one of pleasure; in effect, pain can become pleasurable. Given all this, what is to be trusted as the clear window into reality? Is Plato correct in claiming that all sense impressions are but shadows of reality?

Another approach to this same question is to ask if any interpretation of reality can ever be confirmed as real. After all, an

THE UNICORN PROBLEM

interpretation is pluralistic by definition; there cannot be only one interpretation of an event. If a scientist argues for the reality of the Big Bang as the cause of the universe, and a theologian insists that everything is the handiwork of God, what truth-test should be applied in order to resolve this inconsistency? Logic points to the scientific explanation as true, while most religious doctrines, especially those of Theists, insist that belief in the word of God is preeminent in any and all matters concerned with certain Truth. It then seems that we must pick between two separate versions of reality, one reliant on myths and revelation, and the other claiming to explain the natural world through natural causes alone.

If we say that a proposition, regardless of its specific content (scientific, religious, mystical, etc.) must match reality, by what means are we supposed to know what that reality actually is and when our ideas have "matched" it? All propositions are, by definition, either true or false, but how should the veracity of various proposals be determined? By the means we choose, thereby excluding all the others? How do we know the test for the truth we insist upon actually determines the Truth with a capital T? Most scientists today would argue that all claims about supernatural beings and events are literally nonsense, and all propositions regarding truth must be contained within time and space, i.e., explained as natural events. Yet we could still ask: by what means is *their* truth-bearing claim to be verified?

Any answer given to the question "What is true?" necessarily begs the question, falling into various forms of circular arguments. Examples of this problem are the diverse judgments we make during the course of any day, especially those axiomatic principles and assumptions drawn from inductive reasoning.

Professor Richard M. Gale (1932-2015) states in his book, *On the Philosophy of Religion*: "…attempts to justify induction make use of inductive reasoning when they say that inductive reasoning will continue to work in the future because it has worked in the past. Our beliefs in these framework-constituting principles, therefore, are groundless."

MITCHELL J. FRANGADAKIS

I contend that knowledge in the strict epistemic sense, i.e., not the "can do" kind of knowledge of technology (*techne*) or even the practical type of knowledge Aristotle claimed was necessary when seeking the good life (*phronesis*), but rather the type of knowledge that looks to the cause or origin of things, those very principles by which Reality purportedly operates, this mode of knowledge is not possible through conceptual means. Die-hard rationalists might insist that we haven't put all of the pieces of the Big Picture together as of yet… but their final position seems to be that some day we will; that we are moving ever closer to *certain* Truth because Reality is assembled in a certain way and that way is imminently discoverable. In the same vein as both Pythagoras and Plato, they argue that our Cosmos is mathematically constructed, a divine geometry of sorts, and hence that the essence of existence "out there" is knowable in a final and absolute sense. As the cosmologist Neil deGrasse Tyson (1958-) recently noted, science is solving the so-called mysteries of our existence one by one. Does this mean that at some point we will have explained it all, and that the Theory of Everything will not only reveal itself, it will capture Reality whole, leaving all we deem mysterious behind?

Regardless, we are compelled to ask if any system of knowledge or wisdom – scientific, religious, or even philosophical – has ever offered enough evidence, either empirically or logically, to be absolutely certain of the Truth. It has been amply demonstrated throughout the 2500-year history of Western and Eastern philosophy that there is a counter argument for every truth-claim put forward. If that is the case, we are perforce left to rely on our own judgment, whether or not we consider ourselves well informed, well-educated, or even up to the task. Each of us is left with many profound questions with no unequivocal answers regarding our personal and spiritual lives, at least those that tell us "what is and is not" in any story-ending fashion.

Russell, reflecting on philosophy's inability to answer these same kinds of questions, wrote: "… Has the universe any unity of plan or purpose, or is it a fortuitous concourse of atoms? Is

THE UNICORN PROBLEM

consciousness a permanent part of the universe, giving hope of indefinite growth in "wisdom" or is it a transitory accident on a small planet on which life must ultimately become impossible? Are good and evil of importance to the universe or only to man? Such questions are asked by philosophy, and variously answered by various philosophers. But it would seem that, whether answers be otherwise discoverable or not, the answers suggested by philosophy are none of them 'demonstrably true'..."

Even strident empiricists such as the philosophers John Locke (1632-1704) and David Hume (1711-1776) acknowledged that we don't actually know *facts* about the world. What we call true and factual is simply the relationship of our ideas to one another. If we think rationally, then we can establish what is necessarily true via deduction, but this deductive certainty only reflects the internal harmony of our ideas, not an absolute fact about objective existence. By definition, if an argument is logically sound (the premises are true and the inferences valid), then its conclusion must be true, and this truth is certain. But the facts derived thereby are not necessarily facts about *reality*. They are facts about our ideas, but not certain truths about the independent existence that they purportedly describe. All we have truly demonstrated is the fact that we haven't violated any of the logic rules that determine how the game is to be played in the first place.

Immanuel Kant (1724-1804), extrapolating from Locke's insight, argued that the true nature of the world in and of itself is not knowable...nor will it ever be by mere mortals such as we. We do however construe a world within a few fundamental categories of thought. According to Kant, *time* and *space* are the concepts required in order to think at all, and he referred to these concepts as "synthetic *a priori*." Our mind *processes* the world (in the words of Kant, the mind possesses a "self-activity") and so it is impossible to completely separate reality from mind. In that sense, the nature of existence, the substrate of reality that is believed to be independent of our minds, becomes forever unknowable.

Prior to the time of Kant, the ancient Greek view of

perception was generally accepted without question: external objects emit atoms (in more modern terms, Newtonian *corpuscles*) that stimulate our sense organs. Hence the mind was thought of as a passive receiver, like wax that receives the imprint of a metal key. Kant argues for the proactive nature of the human mind, an insight that he called his own "Copernican Revolution." It is important to note that Kant's establishment of synthetic *a priori* categories was prompted in large part as a response to Hume's radical skepticism that was assaulting the very core of the scientific method.

Kant's revolution was not about our perception of the starry firmament above, but rather of the very process of the human psyche within. Although he was deemed an empiricist, he nonetheless maintained that our existence must be comprehended through categories of understanding that in themselves are necessary and universal, i.e. time and space. For human beings, these categories comprise the foundation – the required format, if you will – of all empirical knowledge. According to Kant, we don't actually perceive time and space; rather, these are the foundational categories of all thoughts – what he referred to as "transcendental intuitions" – without which we could not think at all. Given all this we might conclude that our knowledge of the world is a functional, pragmatic type of knowledge, but not a form of knowledge that is capable of penetrating the mystery of our existence.

If Kant is correct, if the world of concepts (*noumena*) and the world of appearances (*phenomena*) will forever remain misfits, it appears that each of us has been riding one Unicorn or another up to this very moment. We are left with an insoluble division between sensibility and our understanding.

In his *Critique of Pure Reason*, Kant offers us four fundamental claims – his antimonies – that must remain intellectually indeterminable. One example is as follows:

Thesis: There belongs to the world, either as its part or as its cause, a Being that is absolutely necessary.

THE UNICORN PROBLEM

Anti-thesis: An absolutely necessary Being nowhere exists in the world, nor does it exist outside the world as its cause.

He goes on to state: "... the concept of an absolutely necessary Being is a concept of pure reason, that is, a mere Idea the objective reality of which is by no means proved by the fact that reason requires it. That Idea does no more than point to a certain but unattainable completeness, and serves rather to limit the understanding than to extend its sphere." – *Critique of Pure Reason*

Each of his four antinomies point out the obvious: that all truth-bearing claims are embedded with their own refutations and remain, therefore, Unicorns from nose to tail.

***

Advocates of the mystical union with God or a divine source approach the question of Truth from a radically different perspective. Their truth embraces the notion of a transcendent experience beyond time, space, and causation. It is an argument grounded predominantly on personal experiences, and therefore excludes objective, independent verification. In effect, they advocate what is deemed a superior method of knowing, insisting that reason concede to its own limitations.

As William James (1842-1910) points out in his classic book, *The Varieties of Religious Experience*: "Although so similar to states of feeling, mystical states seem to those who experience them to be also states of knowledge. They are states of insight into depths of truth unplumbed by the discursive intellect. They are illuminations, revelations, full of significance and importance, all inarticulate though they remain; and as a rule they carry with them a curious noumenal sense of authority for after-time."

If it is true, however, that *all* rational thought is eclipsed by the mystical experience, we would be forced to conclude that no truth-bearing claims regarding this transcendent realm could be made at all. One might say, for example, that the mystical experience was timeless and infinite, but these judgments would have to be based on intuition or personal feeling alone, not on empirical evidence. It would be more accurate to say that it *felt* or seemed as though it was timeless or infinite to the individual experiencing it. The truths revealed in religious (mystical) experiences remain immediate, and in that way they are similar to dreams, which also possess an immediate sense of meaning, a form of understanding that dissipates once we awaken and mediation begins anew.

It is oftentimes claimed that mystical experiences are indeed the true form of awakening, citing a fundamental type of knowledge or wisdom of which one cannot speak – words necessarily fail to express the essence of the experience. Reality is deemed accessible, but like God must (as some claim) remain ineffable. And if, as a result of some transcendent experience, I insist that God exists (which is not implausible) and you say he does not exist (again, equally plausible), it seems we are both saddled to a Unicorn—and this is a serious problem, replete with cognitive dissonance, or as Existentialists might claim, *false consciousness.*

Nonetheless, if we argue that faith or belief in spiritual revelation remains our ultimate guide to Truth, then we should first consult Soren Kierkegaard (1813-1855) or better yet, Abraham of the Old Testament. What is the lesson there? Faith is necessarily irrational…to an extreme. Until an Angel intervened, Abraham would have sacrificed his only son because he believed God had commanded him to do so. (Schizophrenics oftentimes report hearing similar voices.)

Although there is no direct translation of the concept of faith in Buddhism, I employ this term for the Buddhist practice referred to as *Establishing the View*. In actuality, Buddhist faith begins with critical analysis, wherein a thorough examination of all experiences, mundane or otherwise, is conducted.

"It is essential to doubt, to question all things deeply, to inquire, examine, inspect and experiment … Do not rely on what another says, be they a friend, a monk, a respected teacher or even a sage … Do not rely on what tradition implies, mainstream culture

THE UNICORN PROBLEM

dictates or what scripture may state." – *Gautama Buddha (563-483 B.C.E.)*

Through this process we learn to relinquish our conceptual supports and as is said in Buddhism, leave the raft behind as we step to the other shore. Granted, this may not sound like a recipe for self-assurance or complete certainty, but Buddhists also argue that with enough time and thoughtful examination of our lives a more intuitive form of consciousness gradually evolves within us, a type of knowing that lies beyond analytical thought. Although Vajrayana Buddhists refer to this cognitive shift as *Establishing the View*, I simply refer to this process as an act of faith. Why faith? Because *no external evidence or logic can confirm this reality*.

***

If we look to the past and the ancient Vedas and Upanishads of India (circa 7th-5th century B.C.E.) we find two major metaphysical camps: one with the *Non-Dual view of reality*, and the other with the *Dualist view*. (It should be noted that the metaphysical and ontological doctrine of Buddhism is of the Non-Dual view.) From the Non-Dual orientation, the absolute nature of reality is a whole or unity, a view much like the philosopher Parmenides (5th c. BCE) argued in his time. The parts or particular aspects of our experiences, such as our sense of individuality (egos), prove to be illusions, meaning that they are temporary displays emanating from a universal constant that remains forever the same: Buddha Nature or Dharmakaya for Buddhists, Universal Being for Parmenides, the Brahman of the Vedas, the Eternal Tao of Lao Tzu (c. 600 BCE), or even Plato's Pure Form of the Good. This immutable nature embodies the realm of Truth and Absolute Knowledge, an adamantine realm that undergoes no change, no material degradation, no coming into being or going out of existence. Like the God of our monotheistic traditions, it is perfect in all ways: "that which nothing greater can be conceived," that which remains forever the same and always *is*.

Hence for Buddhist practitioners, the overcoming of the illusory nature of material being and returning to this immutable magisterium is both the initiation into *faith* (as I am employing the term) and the ultimate orientation towards the path to Liberation. To borrow from an old Vedic aphorism, the salt (individuality) is absorbed back into the ocean (unity). Subject and object dissolve into one, and this is only possible because they never were truly separate, as each was always embedded within the other.

This is sometimes referred to as the Mind-Only doctrine, wherein the essential nature of all phenomena is Pure Awareness — absent any determination of personal self-identity — similar in this regard to what occurs in the non-REM periods during deep sleep: no perceptions, no feelings, no sense of being anything at all; yet awareness remains, an essentially content-less reality. Or borrowing from an ancient Taoist aphorism, it remains much like the empty hub at the center of a wheel that allows everything else to revolve around it. Hence from the perspective of Perfection itself, the empty nature of our minds and the nature of external phenomena are non-dual, just like the spokes of the wheel and the empty space in their center are one and the same.

The Dualist school, on the other hand, claims that the spirit of mankind and the absolute spirit of Brahman are distinct. Moreover, they also argue that awareness without an object or content is not possible. Any cognitive act requires some object or event to be aware *of*, and absent this requirement, there is no experience possible. Thus one does not dissolve one's ego back into the unity of the Cosmos at large (Brahman), but rather one realizes the inherently divine nature that surrounds any and all individual instances; one awakens, but without disappearing into a realm of pure emptiness or awareness. There must remain, the Dualists argue, an *enjoyer* of ultimate realization, or else what's the point? Hence the divine nature of reality is worthy of worship and praise in much the same way Theists believe that God is worthy of the same.

In my view, the Non-Dualists are correct in claiming that the essential nature of the Truth Body (in Buddhism, the *Dharmakaya*) is

THE UNICORN PROBLEM

in fact Pure Awareness or Awakened Mind. This is a realm of ultimate simplicity that requires no objectivity in order to be what it is, in the same way that God's essential attributes in our monotheistic traditions are described as simplicity, immateriality, and immutability…in effect, beyond all measure. However, at the same time we are more than capable of realizing this empty nature while still remaining within these temporary (illusory) experiences we call human existence, since this constant condition of Pure Awareness is always present, even in the most mundane of circumstances.

Nonetheless, in this instance we have a 4,500 year-old argument over whether Ultimate Reality is Dualistic or Non-Dual Monism. One might expect that an argument such as this could be resolved, that practitioners and yogis on the Vedic or the Buddhist path would resolve this metaphysical problem definitively at some point…but it hasn't happened. In a like manner, there are major ontological and epistemological disagreements between various philosophical schools, East and West. Some schools, for example, claim that objects exist independently of our minds (Realists or Materialists). Others (Idealists) claim that existence is to some degree an illusion or a construct of our minds. In regard to an experience as intimate as the nature of our own minds and perceptions, how is it that we have reached such an impasse? I would say that in this regard, we are staring straight into the eyes of a very old and very large Unicorn.

It is useful if not absolutely required that in our ongoing search for certain Truth, we become acquainted with the many aspects of The Unicorn Problem(s), which I have summarized in the following list:

> 1) Definitions: Is it possible to actually define anything? Does a definition actually reveal what a thing is – its essence – or do definitions simply function as placeholders upon which to place our own beliefs? How might we define with complete precision the meaning of the words "good" or "bad" or "religion?" Even more difficult is the definition of that which all of us experience daily: consciousness. What

about those concepts we hold most dear, such as truth, knowledge, and justice?

2) The Infinite Regress Problem: Every claim requires justification of some sort if we have any confidence in reason at all. In legal or formal arguments, we would say that claims require evidence (warrants), reasons for why we should accept the claims as true or reject them as false. But how do we justify as true the very premises we employ in our arguments? Don't they require evidence as well?

3) What constitutes a self-evident Truth or a clear and distinct idea? Are there any brute facts that require no justification? If so, is this the same as claiming the superiority of common sense, or should we attribute our ability to know truth when we hear it to our strictly rational nature? (See #2 above – similar issues).

4) The Problem of Falsifiability in contemporary science (This will be discussed in more detail in Chapter III).

5) Logical Paradoxes. If conclusions that are 100% certain are only available through deductive reasoning, which are affirmed by the very rules of logic, then how is it that we are able to formulate logically deductive certainties that contradict one another? Zeno's paradoxes, Bertrand Russell's "class of all classes," and Immanuel Kant's antimonies are examples of this problem. Furthermore, if pure logic provides one kind of truth but our sense fields inform us of something different, upon which of these forms of knowledge should we rely? The simplest example is the movement of the sun in our sky, and the obvious discrepancy between what appears to us each sunny day and what scientific knowledge reveals as fact.

6) The Faith/Reason Divide. If it is Truth in an absolute sense that we desire, where should we take refuge? If we

conclude that reason bears inherent restraints that prevent us from reaching this level of Truth, that the dualistic nature of rational thought leaves us short of an absolute fact, then is faith the true solution? If faith rejects reason, in principle at least, then can faith-based belief systems offer rational advice regarding what is real and certain…or not? Does faith have the right to give reasonable arguments as to why the Truth that faith reveals should be accepted as such?

7) The implicit, self-referencing nature of all epistemic arguments. If a scientist, for example, insists that all knowledge claims regarding reality must be grounded in space/time, where exactly in space/time is that Truth justified?

8) *Aporia*/The "knowing of not knowing." What positive value, if any, might this Socratic impasse present, or is this the dead-end that awaits all human attempts at certain Truth?

9) The Gods or the Earth Giants? This is Plato's way of asking if there is an absolute Truth or whether man truly is the measure of all things. This issue remains intellectually indeterminable to this day.

10) And, as a consequence of all of the above, the moral conundrums each of us face each day … where do we find the right answers to those problems of the utmost gravity? This is perhaps the alpha Unicorn, and I will discuss it more fully in the last chapter: *Embracing Doubt / Life Without Unicorns.*

As Bertrand Russell points out: "…all our knowledge of truths is infected with some degree of doubt, and a theory which ignored this fact would be plainly wrong." If we claim to know reality in any final or absolute sense, as most religious doctrines claim to do, then those truth-claims must demonstrate in some manner that what is asserted as definitely true and what is actually the *case* are synonymous. But that demonstration unfortunately does not seem possible, and we are only capable of determining what is *not* the case. The actual nature of reality and our human condition remain open questions, and we might hope that *certain* Truth would stand naked and self-evident before us as a brute fact that is undeniable – yet our experience of that Truth bounds compulsively from one possibility to another, like a Unicorn freed from its tether.

CHAPTER 2
WHAT SHOULD WE BELIEVE?

"Is it not strange that ignorance and complaisance are stronger than wisdom?"
Marcus Aurelius (121-180 AD)

PLATO'S ALLEGORY OF THE CAVE

Imagine a cave filled with prisoners chained to a wall, forever condemned to perceive what amounts to little more than illusions in front of them, mesmerizing shadows cast from fires behind them. Because they are chained, they have no way of realizing the deception that is being played on them. This is the only reality they have ever known.

Ultimately, a young man is able to break free from the chains. (The actual Greek term here literally means to "turn about"; enlightenment in Eastern spiritual traditions is oftentimes referred to as a turning about at the deepest seat of consciousness). Spotting a faint light in the distance, he locates steps carved into the rock and escapes the darkness of the cave. Once outside, the overbearing light of the sun shocks him. What he believed was illumination in the cave, but a small fire that projected the shadows, is now revealed as illusion. He was seeing the true light for the first time, the light of the Sun, Plato's symbol of the ultimate Good and the source of true knowledge, or First Principle.

After a time, he acclimates to his new conditions, basking in the glow of his ultimate realization. Soon enough, however, he realizes what he now has to do; he feels obliged by an innate moral duty to free the others. He returns to the darkness and illusions of the cave, as might a prophet returning from the high desert in order to save his confused people, proclaiming the way out. His fellow prisoners listen to him but ultimately resist his admonitions, and quickly pronounce him deluded. Angered by his unceasing calls to wisdom, the prisoners kill him.

A GATHERING OF UNICORNS

In our quest for abiding answers to our existential questions, each of us must take that first step out of the cave of our own illusions in order to know the truth of what we experience as our reality. Plato (428-348 BCE) understood the courage and effort required in our escape from that kind of darkness, yet he was convinced that complete and certain Knowledge was indeed possible for each of us. He argues that Pure Ideas (Forms) lie beyond the enclosure of our beliefs and opinions, overreaching our very sense fields, a realm that can only be apprehended through reason and the dialectic. We might be inclined to call them "ideals," but for Plato they are that and much more. *Pure Forms* are the true Reality of our existence; the rest are but shadows and reflections.

In his *Republic* Plato speaks to our need for Justice. As a society we strive for just laws and fair social arrangements. Unfortunately, the wild appetites and deep pathos of humanity belie the very notion of actual Justice, for the world we experience in our daily lives is anything but fair and equitable. No, the purity of actual Justice resides above our earth-bound laws, always inspiring us to overcome the innate shortcomings of our legal and social systems. Ultimately, through a disciplined practice of the dialectic inspired by the faculty of wisdom itself, we may come to know the Pure Form of the Good, the real source of Justice, Truth and Beauty.

Thus, for Plato Truth resides beyond all phenomena and Reality can only be found deep within the principles and internal laws (the divine *Logos*) that organize and regulate the realm of any and all appearances. I will argue that this same Platonic Good is that which was sought by our early Church fathers when they prayed for "union with God."

The Neo-Platonist Plotinus (204-270CE) held that the Platonic Good and the monotheistic notion of the One were synonymous: "The three basic principles of Plotinus' metaphysics are called by him 'the One' (or, equivalently, 'the Good'), Intellect, and Soul (see V1; V 9.). These principles are both ultimate ontological realities and explanatory principles…The One is the absolutely simple first principle of all. It is both 'self-caused' and the cause of being for everything else in the universe." – *S.E.P.*

This notion of the Good (although not necessarily referred to in the same manner) is also the goal of Buddhist meditative absorptions (*Absolute Bodhicitta or Awakened Nature*). As Edward Conze (1904-1979) explains in his book, *Buddhism: its Essence and Development:* "We are told that Nirvana is permanent, stable, imperishable, immoveable, ageless, deathless, unborn, and unbecome, that it is power, bliss and happiness, the secure refuge, the shelter and the place of unassailable security; that it is the real Truth and the supreme Reality; that it is the good, the supreme goal and the one and only consummation of our life, the eternal, hidden and incomprehensible Peace."

Pivoting to a more pragmatic level, the Good was the essence of Socrates' (470-399 BCE) counsel when he insisted that the wise person would rather suffer harm than intentionally harm another. Why? Because to intentionally harm another forsakes our knowledge of this primordial Good.

In her delightful book, *Plato at the Googleplex*, philosopher Rebecca Newberger Goldstein (1950-) summarizes Plato's appraisal of the Good in this way: "To live the life worth living one must be able to grasp and internalize the goodness that makes the cosmos worth the existing. One must integrate the beautiful proportionality of the character of the physical universe into one's own moral character, and then, and only then, will one see oneself in relation to all else — and all others — in the right perspective, the distortions of the cave corrected."

For Buddhists, Wisdom (Greek: *Sophia*) abides as the natural expression of the human heart when it remains attuned to a class of knowledge and truth that supersedes explanations or conceptual foundations, free as well from the emotional fetters of fear or hope. Wisdom, it is said, may be embraced in the natural openness or emptiness within every thought, feeling, and physical expression that a human being can possibly engender. Since this open and empty nature is our essence, it must be (as Socrates might advise) r*ecollected*. The overriding notion is that all realms of existence, regardless of specific content, participate in this openness — albeit unrealized. Thus, I also contend that the ultimate goal of Buddhist meditation and the examined life of Socrates and his student Plato circle their way back to the origin or A*rche'*, the Pure Form of the Good from which all else emanates.

Aristotle (384-322 BCE), who was Plato's student, would later adopt this same approach and claim that what constitutes the good life is a state of *flourishing*. This human flourishing (*eudemonia*) is only possible when our potential as human beings is fulfilled, when we progress from our potentiality to full actuality. Since Aristotle defined human beings as "the rational animal", developing the faculty of reason is a key element of this good life. Thus, when Socrates, the citizen-hero of Plato's allegory, proclaimed over two thousand years ago, "The unexamined life is not worth living", perhaps his admonition was not only correct but was also required. He was extolling a practical truth that he believed was timeless and universal: If we are interested in living a good life, a flourishing life, a heroic life of personal integrity, and ultimately a happy life, it is essential that we examine that life as we are living it.

So, we should ask ourselves in true Socratic fashion: What exactly is an examined life?

First of all, if we claim to have learned anything from our ancient sages, a life lived in this way is a constant vigil of sorts and must be cultivated with a specific intention and reflected upon in an honest and purposeful manner. An examined life is the contemplative life wherein little or nothing is taken for granted and a strong sense of skepticism is actually encouraged. It is one in which our assumptions about truth, knowledge and reality are subject to critical reviews on our internal witness stand, to be questioned and cross-examined for their veracity in our lives. Buddhists might refer to this manner of examination as "mindfulness practice" or moreover, as taking full advantage of our "precious human re-birth."

Socrates urges us to live a life wherein we are compelled to understand the meaning, or possible lack thereof, of our actions and our existence. An honest self-examination to this degree may force us to revise or abandon our most cherished beliefs, opinions, and judgments – and their revision and reintegration into our lives can be a slow and painful process. In this way we should keep in mind that the sages of old warned that even Zeus, the supreme 'god' of Olympus, must suffer in order to gain knowledge. As Plato explains it, the examined life is where virtue and knowledge cross paths and are both directed by *agathon*, the universal Good that makes life worth living.

It is a given then that wisdom is hard-earned and requires at least a modicum of critical thinking skills and an application of reason in the most efficient and straightforward manner possible. These are skills that can be – and certainly should be – taught as a requirement in any educational curriculum.

In this regard however, the following example from the Texas Republican Party platform of 2012 reminds us of the impediments that stand in the way of humankind's progress towards that goal: "We oppose the teaching of Higher Order Thinking Skills… critical thinking skills and similar programs that are simply a relabeling of Outcome-Based Education (OBE) (mastery learning) which focus on behavior modification and have the purpose of challenging the student's fixed beliefs and undermining parental authority."

Aside from the Orwellian nature of this platform, understanding the rationale for this stance is challenging. Overall, we are left with the difficulty of separating moral values from social and fiscal policies, and we could question whether or not this is even possible. After all, if the Supreme Court of the United States can proclaim that money equals free speech, then the school board's position almost seems rational.

In 1784 the philosopher Immanuel Kant (1724-1804) wrote a widely published essay titled *What Is Enlightenment?* He answers this question in the first sentence of the essay. "Enlightenment," he says, "is man's emergence from his self-incurred immaturity." And how is this to be accomplished? By cultivating the very skills the Texas school board is trying to eliminate from our educational curriculum.

The thrust of Kant's essay stresses the need for independent thought, which is the capacity to think for oneself, independent of dogma, propaganda, and fossilized systems of belief. We become enlightened thinkers when we question the basis of our judgments, when we try to uncover their origins and address the assumptions upon which our views depend. Authority, no matter its source – be it parental, governmental, or clerical – must be questioned. We cannot accept a given truth blindly, without reason, without the essential ability to think critically. This was Kant's position (and the Buddha's), knowing full well the difficulty involved in consistently enacting it and how much personal courage was required in order to become – and remain – an independent thinker. Kant lived by this motto: "Dare to be wise!"

Although we may not fully understand the process, the acquisition of knowledge begins early in life. There are some elementary sources upon which we all depend to make any claims to knowledge at all. We are all, for example, influenced by the culture and the language system in which we are reared and by the traditional values and beliefs of that culture. In addition we are taught, as are all children in all cultures, to respect and honor our traditions and the authority figures within them. To a large extent the purpose of an educational system is to transmit those traditions and values from one generation to the next. So we can partially understand the motive of the aforementioned Texas Board in this way: they want to preserve what they deem to be a system of traditional values. The problem now is defining the phrase *traditional values*, which seems more a product of magical thinking than critical thinking.

With the possible exception of scientific principles, what we call knowledge in any area of study is constantly changing. This is especially true in such diverse fields as medicine, mental health, education, media, and even economics. In the Western intellectual traditions of today the possibility of error in anyone's truth-claims is pretty much assumed, which is to say that the truths currently accepted are seen as provisional truths, not the big, capital "T" kind of Truth that the ancient theologians and philosophers were seeking.

Russell puts it this way: "Is there any knowledge in the world which is so certain that no reasonable man could doubt it? This question, which at first sight might not seem difficult, is really one of the most difficult that can be asked."

Even science must acknowledge its own track record, realizing that the laws or governing principles in physics today may be revised or even abandoned tomorrow. Science, it has been noted, has a *historicity*: any claims about *timeless, universal, necessary and certain Truth*, Truth about which it would be *impossible* to be wrong, is not supported by the empirical evidence thus far. The Indian philosopher K.C. Bhattacharya (1875-1949) went so far as to define modern science as "the correction of error," and scientists of today generally comport themselves with this attitude in mind. There is little chance that contemporary scientists would make the same mistake as Galileo (1564-1642). His calculations contradicted the Church's long-standing position that human beings are special creations, residing as we do in the center of the Cosmos just the way God planned it. Although Galileo believed he had unearthed timeless, universal, and certain facts about the world, indirectly revealing how insignificant we might be, his reality contradicted that of the Holy powers. His reward was house arrest. Today, scientists have no problem positing provisional or relative truths, never claiming that a scientific theory is 100% certain. They claim no Theory of Everything…not yet, anyway.

***

THE UNICORN PROBLEM

In keeping with the research of the mythologist Joseph Campbell (1904-1987), we could address our quest for the examined life as embarking on the Hero's Journey. As the myths describe, this is a personal odyssey we all must undertake in probing our own alignment to the truths by which we live. For the mystic Gurdjieff (1872-1949) the goal of the human quest was the achievement of the ancient Greek notion of "perfection" or self-mastery. (In Buddhism the final stage of awakening is oftentimes referred to as "The Great Perfection"). This mandate for human fulfillment necessarily requires us to abide in a more complete state of consciousness, or at least to realize that the core of our consciousness is indeed purity itself — what Plato, as mentioned earlier, termed the Good. But to do so we must overcome the impediments and challenges that reside within our own psyches. And inevitably, we must ask ourselves: is this type of wisdom even possible for such obviously imperfect creatures as ourselves?

Can we honestly sustain those rare moments of insight, those peak moments when we realize that perfection is indeed a presence within us? Is it possible to overcome the cognitive barriers we all share as participants in the human condition? Can we sustain this level of experience for a lifetime? Every wisdom-seeker knows how difficult it is to change the long-ingrained habits of his or her body, speech and mind, and how frequently each of us fails to live the ideal of a conscientiously examined life.

Aldous Huxley (1894-1963), the English novelist and a fervent agnostic, who in the last quarter-century of his life, found his own orientation to Truth through mysticism, claimed that our purpose in life was to seek union with the divine ground of all Being, i.e. that which many might call God. He also claimed that all doctrines, be they philosophical, religious, or scientific in scope will necessarily be incomplete, the necessary outcome of "dualistic thinking." "Words are good servants," he said, "but bad masters." Concepts possess what is referred to as a "suppressed correlative." The mental categories we generate depend on their opposites in order to have any meaning at all: the light depends on darkness to be known, what is high requires what is low, all objects demand a subject, a "1" (something) discovers its meaning through the concept of "0" (nothing). And any claims regarding what is good remain completely dependent on what is deemed its refutation in order to possess any value for us.

In this way, Huxley is very close to the Buddhist view regarding thinking in general and conceptuality in particular. Dualistic thought in Buddhism is deemed capable of *relative truth* only, a realm constricted to measurements and comparisons, of contrasting one concept with another and understanding the relationship of one category to the next. If this is indeed the case, then the value of dualistic thought remains practical at best, and necessarily relative to the particular circumstances in which we find ourselves; all truth becomes a conditioned truth, a provisional or relative understanding. The big T kind of Truth, the kind of Truth that Buddhists describe as empty of any essence or self-inherent being, is reserved for what I will loosely refer to as Religious Experiences—a direct cognition only available through introspection and meditation practices (Religious experiences are addressed in more detail later in this text).

Buddhist ontology, however, does take the issue one step further and suggest that our ordinary cognitive functions are binary as well. The act of thinking for example is not simply conceptually dualistic but is also experientially dualistic: we have a thought…then not; and the cycle repeats indefinitely. Buddhism advances the momentary and thereby essentially transitory view of existence, every instant dissolving into the next. In point of fact, a "moment" is merely another concept, useful in mathematics or physics, but not a reality of our experiences. Bertrand Russell adopts an analogous view, suggesting that our primary mistake in understanding the nature of matter or substance is to assume that it is continuous or naturally persistent, when the actual fabric of reality may be transitory in nature —present and not present in the very same instant.

In Buddhist teachings, the "not thinking" part of the meditation cycle is the open space between our thoughts. According to Buddhist doctrine this emptiness or simple openness is in need of recognition if we are to put the fundamental pieces of our minds back together again. The unity realized in this instance is between being and non-being, coeval aspects of all ordinary thoughts and perceptions.

As the Buddhist Saint and yogi Milarepa (1052-1135) put it:

"...Since appearance in the form of existing substance and reality which is non-existing emptiness are essentially inseparable and of a single savor, there is not just the intrinsic awareness or extrinsic awareness, but a vast coalescence of everything."

For Huxley and many others like him, this divine union with the sacred ground of all is an *intuitive* enterprise, not a logical one; hopping rides on various trains of thought will not take us to our desired destination. In fact, It is remarkable how many of the deepest, most rationally-oriented thinkers in our Western traditions – regardless of religious backgrounds – influential thinkers like Socrates, Plato, Baruch Spinoza, Bishop Berkeley, Immanuel Kant, Friedrich Hegel, Goethe, and many others – have drawn similar conclusions. They claim or infer that there is a Universal Truth, an abiding *certainty* that is accessible to all those who are willing to become the Hero of their own lives by genuinely comprehending their human condition.

As Jean Paul Sartre (1905-1980) stated so succinctly, each of us is "condemned to be free." Ultimately this means that each of us is alone in our search to find some meaning, purpose and value in our individual and collective lives, and that each of us is free to draw our own conclusions, even if our judgments lead us astray. This in large part is why there is such comfort in the idea of an abiding Universal Truth, an Invisible Big Mind, and an Ultimate Reality that abides as Perfection itself, for it holds the key to the enigma of why we are here at all.

Every religion invokes its own theory of this Ultimate Reality and hence, the ultimate meaning of life itself (metaphysics), of knowledge and truth and the means by which they are obtained (epistemology), of the essence of human existence (ontology), and ultimately of what constitutes a virtuous life – what Buddhists,

Hindus, Jews, Christians, and Muslims might translate as the notion of "righteousness" and what philosophers refer to as the study of ethics. The righteous path of Buddhism, for example, is composed of the Paramitas (virtues), which includes admonitions regarding right livelihood, right understanding, right conduct, right meditation, the need for honesty, perseverance...and so on. These are deemed the moral virtues necessary for liberation. All religions ponder similar issues and then, despite the general differences between the various doctrines, proceed to answer these existential questions in surprisingly similar fashion.

Nevertheless there persists a significant split between the Big Picture of religion and the more sense-oriented or empirical view of reality held by many philosophical systems, most especially contemporary science. At the heart of this division lies the argument over the origin of existence in general, and of human existence in particular, as well as the radical differences in the answers given when asked: "What does it mean to know something?" These distinct magisteria, one grounded in the supernatural and the other a purely naturalistic orientation, are two independent approaches to solving the same mystery. Scientists, philosophers and religious adepts address the same perennial problems that each generation must face, consciously or unconsciously. They can be summarized as the questions of "who, what, where, when, and why?" of our personal and collective existence.

Who, for example, are we? What does it mean to be a human being? What exactly is the human condition? How is the individual different from the society in which she finds herself, or should we look first to the society in order to understand the individual? Have we been created in God's image, or are we the natural but random product of an evolving planet and universe? It is surprising how many individuals claim to know the answer to these types of questions.

We might ask if it is it true, as the pre-Socratic philosopher, Democritus (c. 460-370 BCE) maintained, that we are but *atoms and the void* and nothing else? How does this explanation square with the

THE UNICORN PROBLEM

spontaneous arising of phenomena, as promulgated in Buddhist doctrine? Are we souls who have temporarily inhabited a corporeal body, glued in some mysterious fashion to the inner workings of blood, flesh, bones—and a modicum of gray matter? Then again, perhaps we are strictly corporeal bodies who only imagine, as the psychologist Gilbert Ryle (1900-1976) observed, that there be "ghosts in the machine?"

When I speak of myself, is there actually a 'self' within me who listens? Hume argues that there was no self to be found when he looked within, but rather only an endlessly fleeting bundle of perceptions and images. And, that what we call *self* is little more than an imaginary band wrapped around constantly moving appearances – the flux of internal phenomena – to which we addend the general concept of "I."

Buddhists would agree with Hume, advocating a non-dual selfless view of personal identity. In Buddhism, even though all entities are dependent on a process of aggregation or accretion of primary elements, there is no essence to these elements: there is no self-inherent being – no primary substance – in anything, including us. This is why all phenomena are deemed empty of any intrinsic nature in Buddhist ontology. No matter what we imagine ourselves to be, the self is ultimately without form or substance (Sanskrit: *sunya*). Both schools, of thought – that of Hume and that of Buddhist ontology – advance what is generally termed in philosophy as the *Illusory Theory of Self*, a position to which most contemporary philosophers subscribe.

And are we basically ego-driven, thinking of little else beyond self-survival, or can we claim to be a higher link in the Great Chain of Being, somewhere between animal and angel? And if higher, do we have a center, a 'soul' or essence? If so, where exactly is it? Is it in our brain or in our heart? Is there an existence "out there," or do we simply construe reality from moment to moment within ourselves? Or are we, as Buddhists might claim, mere temporary embodiments of a universal and ultimately compassionate Big Mind?

In their book *Ten Theories of Human Nature*, Stevenson and

Habermon survey the various perspectives on these issues, including those offered by Confucius, the Upanishad of Hinduism, The Bible, Buddhism, Plato, Aristotle, Kant, Marx, Sartre, and finally Darwinian evolution.

The authors claim that all of these various philosophies and religious traditions offer the following:

1) A metaphysical understanding of the universe and humanity's place in it;

2) A theory of human nature in the narrower sense of some distinctive general claims about human beings, the human society, and the human condition;

3) A diagnosis of some typical defect in human beings, of what tends to go wrong in human life society;

4) And, finally, a prescription or ideal for how human life should best be lived, typically offering guidance to individuals and human societies.

Unfortunately, adherents of any particular belief system or ideology tend to close the door on outside criticisms of their particular convictions. Stevenson and Habermon claim that the usual response towards unbelievers – those who hold beliefs and convictions contrary to our own – is twofold: first, don't allow any evidence to count against the theory or ideology, i.e. don't *allow one's beliefs to be falsified*. Most belief systems adopt the view that counterevidence or defeaters for their claims can and should be explained away and thereby dismissed. Secondly, if criticized, question the motives of the critics in terms of the theory or ideology itself. This tactic often takes advantage of the logical fallacy referred to as "argumentum ad hominem," or "argument against the person," an aspect of rhetoric or informal logic. In this instance, if all else fails in an argument, attack the integrity and character of your critic.

Regardless of whether we are addressing the specific views of

THE UNICORN PROBLEM

Marxism, Darwinism, or Buddhism, if an ideology is indeed a closed system – if no refutations are allowed, Stevenson and Habermon argue that the Socratic dialectic offers us a viable alternative to the problem. For those who might object to a rational approach to the experience of belief or faith, the authors also point out that Jesus was willing to argue seriously with anyone – social outcasts or Rabbis included.

Stevenson and Habermon continue by saying: "…Everybody has to have some sort of theory of human nature or ideology or philosophy to live by; you must have some conceptions of what affects human well-being, and some views about what is not worth doing – even if only about what your own long-term well-being or happiness consists in…No human being who lives at a more than animal level can completely opt out of offering reasons for his or her beliefs and actions."

***

Many people might insist that the best response to the human condition is simply to get on with it. We should stop lingering on life's big mysteries and instead put our attention where it will do the most good. Wondering about the source, function, or purpose of human consciousness, for example, might be an interesting intellectual pastime for some, but it doesn't do the dishes, buy new tennis shoes for the kids, or spring bail for the errant uncle in the family. Consciousness should concern itself with problems it can solve or at least attempt to solve, instead of wasting its time on confusing puzzles and Rorschach guessing games. The very act of consciousness trying to solve itself seems absurd: is this the function that consciousness should have? Is this what consciousness is for, becoming an interlocutor to its own nature, grilling itself in hopes of a true and honest answer? Can we ever understand how knowing happens? These may be intriguing questions to some, but why be concerned with the merely speculative or hypothetical? Why not focus on the true necessities of our daily lives – food, shelter, and safety? Aren't these the real problems and don't they also demand some concrete solutions that each of us is willing to accept?

These last words are the arguments of the predominantly practical person. I would at least soften the stridency of that practical attitude by noting that both philosophy (within which I would include modern science) and religion are necessarily more contemplative by their very nature. A contemplative outlook is quite natural for those persons who find meaning by stepping back from life's necessities and letting his or her sense of wonder and intuition lead the way. While a pragmatic person may simply grow impatient waiting for water to boil, the scientist wonders why water turns to steam when the kettle gets hot.

And where most of us might simply be enjoying a bright sun in a clear blue sky, the scientist wonders why the sky is blue, while the natural philosopher ruminates on the true movement of the sun and stars as opposed to how things appear to us. Meanwhile the epistemologist muses on the nature of Truth and whether or not it can ever be known, and the religious adept asks perhaps the most difficult of these basic questions: *Why do I suffer?*

As to the last question, I contend that the discipline of philosophical contemplation and the examined life is a probe in the right direction; that is, towards a consistent attitude adjustment that slowly alleviates our personal distress. Moreover we should keep in mind that from the philosophical viewpoint, the questions asked may be more important than the answers given. That is not to say that particular proposals or doctrines of religious and philosophical camps are meaningless. Obviously they are very important to those who believe the claims made within those particular disciplines. Philosophy, however, focuses more on the *means* by which those answers are derived. Philosophy is more the vehicle than the destination.

In the categories of metaphysics, ontology, epistemology, and ethics, the questions themselves hold the high ground in any argument. The responses to these issues seem to swerve dramatically according to time, place, circumstance, and the individual or groups

THE UNICORN PROBLEM

concerned. We could insist, for example, that the genius of Plato is not so much in the answers he offered, but rather in the questions he had the courage and wisdom to ask. Even in science, or I should say, especially in science, the same questions throughout the millennia of human history have generated a vast array of possible solutions, but the actual problems that generated these solutions have remained fundamentally unchanged.

For example, our understanding of the earth, sun and moon has gone through various *paradigm shifts*, a term first coined by the philosopher, Thomas Kuhn (1922-1996). In his 1962 book titled *The Structure of Scientific Revolution*, Kuhn states that our human advances in scientific knowledge are a "series of peaceful interludes punctuated by intellectually violent revolutions." In a paradigm shift one picture of the Universe supplants another. For example, the Newtonian model of a uniform space and a constant measure of time is changed into the Einsteinianan view of curved space and relative time. In the field of physics that's a radical shift.

We also now know that the earth is not flat...nor is it stable, for that matter. Huge tectonic plates are constantly shifting beneath us, responding to the 6000-degree heat at the earth's core and the fact that we are spinning round the earth's axis at 1000 miles per hour. A map of California from 1665 shows the Golden State as an island. It could very well end up that way sometime in the future, but for now it remains connected to the rest of the continent. As for the sun, we used to believe that the heat it produced was a purely chemical process, whereas we now know that atomic fusion is the actual source of the sun's power. What the sun *is* has changed – its essence redefined – and the long-held belief that it was the chariot of Apollo and that its fire is extinguished at night only to be rekindled at daybreak has definitely fallen out of favor. Knowledge and the answers it provides are always on the move, which is enough to make sober-minded individuals wonder if the philosophers', theologians', and mystics' quest for certainty is wasting what little precious time is afforded them.

No doubt maintaining a practical attitude towards our lives is both necessary and wise. As the saying goes: 'Trust in Allah, but tie up your camel.' But a practical attitude alone doesn't go far enough; it is shortsighted, too cave-like, and if we focus on practical affairs too intensely, we limit our perception and understanding of our essential tasks here on earth and their relative importance to our physical and mental well-being. The real challenge is to see the necessities of our lives as only a segment of the whole of our existential concerns and possibilities, a partial rendering of the Big Picture each of us must comprehend, such that our focus is reoriented towards the questions that have challenged all humans throughout the generations, no matter in what time, place, or circumstance – from Adam and Eve to the present moment.

CHAPTER 3
IN PURSUIT OF TRUTH

"What is the first business of he who philosophizes? To throw away self-conceit. For it is impossible for a man to begin to learn that which he thinks he knows."
Epictetus (A.D. 55-135?)

"Once upon a time two explorers came upon a clearing in the jungle. In the clearing were growing many flowers and many weeds. One explorer says, 'Some gardener must tend this plot.' The other disagrees, 'There is no gardener.'
"So they pitch their tents and set a watch. No gardener is ever seen. 'But perhaps he is an invisible gardener.' So they set up a barbed-wire fence. They electrify it. They patrol with bloodhounds. But no shrieks ever suggest that some intruder has received a shock. No movements of the wire ever betray an invisible climber. The bloodhounds never give cry.
"Yet still the believer is not convinced. 'But there is a gardener, invisible, intangible, insensitive to electric shocks, a gardener who has no scent and makes no sound, a gardener who comes secretly to look after the garden which he loves.' At last the Skeptic despairs, 'but what remains of your original assertion? Just how does what you call an invisible, intangible, eternally elusive gardener differ from an imaginary gardener or even from no gardener at all?"
Antony Flew (1923-2010)

THE UNICORN PROBLEM

HOW TO RECOGNIZE A UNICORN

In the thought experiment above, the first explorer is what many of us might refer to as a "true believer." Her experiences in the world lead her to believe that the truth of her convictions is self-evident. Thus, she refuses to accept any amount of evidence suggesting she might be wrong about the Gardener. She is assured of her conclusion beyond any doubt. The result is that her conviction can never be proven false. No matter how many times the assumed Gardener fails to arrive, this Explorer will never stand corrected and admit that there might be other explanations for the wondrous surround of flowers in which she finds herself that there may be inferred a more conclusive explanation (adduction). In her mind, there is always one more test to be performed... ad infinitum. It is for this very reason that modern science insists that any scientific theory must be in some manner falsifiable. Popper's Falsifiability Theorem states that any hypothesis or theory must have a means available to prove it false. If I contend, for example, that all swans are white, then the discovery of a black swan would clearly demonstrate that the claim is refuted, and this is exactly what happened to all the logicians who at one time used the major premise "all swans are white" as an example of a universal truth. Popper's theorem is one of the primary cognitive instruments that science employs in its search for truth.

Thus, the fundamental reason why the Intelligent Design argument in theology (which Flew's Thought Experiment is addressing) does not qualify as a scientific theory is because it can never be demonstrated as false. Due to some logistical complications —what is known as the error of affirming the consequent in deductive reasoning – science insists that there has to be some way of proving an idea false if it is to have any scientific cachet. If a person absolutely believes in Intelligent Design, no amount of evidence will change his or her mind. A conscientious scientist expects to have a change of mind as often as the evidence requires it. In other words, from a scientific perspective, how would one go about demonstrating Intelligent Design to be untrue? If physical evidence won't do, what will? There have been countless examples in archeology, biology, chemistry, and so forth that have confirmed Darwin's theory of evolution. Yet, what a conscientious scientist asks is: If Darwin's Theory is true, what result should *not* occur? If the unwanted results do occur, then the theory is in need of revision, or perhaps must be thrown out altogether. In the deductive logic that science depends on, affirming the consequent of a hypothetical proposition is not justification of a certain outcome, but rather only the approbation of a likely truth.

For example, if I know that rain causes the little creek by my cabin to rise, then the following statement (a hypothetical syllogism) can be made: *If it rains, then the creek will rise.* The rule regarding conclusions we make when working with hypothetical syllogisms – a form of logic we necessarily employ throughout any ordinary day in order to function as a normal human being – is to "affirm the antecedent" or "deny the consequent." This is the only way to reach a *certain* conclusion. If I observe that the creek rose and then claim that the rain caused it, I am committing a logical fallacy: there could be other reasons why the creek rose. Perhaps the damn up-stream burst? We can't be certain of the cause. But if I say the creek didn't rise, then I can be certain that it didn't rain – i.e., I have denied the consequent (The classic example in Eastern philosophy of this type of hypothetical syllogism is as follows: if smoke, then fire; there is smoke, therefore there must be fire).

Therefore, in regard to Darwin's theory of evolution, just because we get the results we expected (analogous to the creek rising or the occurrence of smoke) doesn't mean the theory is completely certain. Other causes may explain the same results. These deductive conclusions pose a serious problem in science, since positive results do not necessarily prove one's theory or hypothesis, at least not in any absolute sense. There is no amount of empirical evidence that can prove a scientific theory to be absolutely true.

Given all this, we can say with certitude, i.e. by definition, that the theory of Intelligent Design is not a valid scientific theory. It is a

THE UNICORN PROBLEM

belief or conviction that one refuses to abandon. Those who argue that it should stand side by side with Darwin's theory of evolution in a science class don't understand the scientific method of inquiry or the fundamentals of logic.

This is but one example of the innumerable ways in which the habits and conscious operations of our minds lead us into confusion, where lazy thinking and emotional biases conspire against a clear understanding of our circumstances. As a more ordinary example, let's imagine a scenario in which a friend reports to you that he has just met the most wonderful person: she's intelligent, funny, and an immensely compassionate person. What's wrong with your friend's judgment about this woman?

It is simply this: your friend's conclusion is not justified. Obviously, one cannot conclude from one brief encounter with a person the general character and intelligence of that person. This is an example of what is commonly referred to as a hasty generalization. An old Zen aphorism states that if you want to actually know a person, you must live with him or her for a year, and then draw your generalizations. You will have a lot more information to work with, and your conclusions will more likely prove relevant.

In philosophy we wonder: when we make a declaration, offer a proposal, determine claims to be either true or false, what do we mean? How do we know this? How do we justify these positions? Simply put, philosophy is most interested in the *assumptions* any particular subject matter rests upon, the underlying and oftentimes unconscious platforms of our thoughts and judgments.

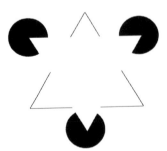

If I were to ask you how many triangles do you see in this image, what would your answer be?

If you take a moment to actually count the number of triangles, you will see that there are none. No triangles present in the image. But since I asked: *How many* triangles? The underlying assumption is that triangles are present. A better, less biased way of asking this question would have been: *Are there* any triangles in this image? If I had asked this first, then the correct answer would have been more readily at hand.

If we are reflective souls, which is to say, if we are philosophical in our outlook, then perhaps the most important question we can ask ourselves is this: Are we asking the right questions? Philosophers do their best to answer this by eliminating their own biases, prejudices, and assumptions right from the start. Whether this is even possible has been a matter of philosophical discussion from the time of Socrates to this day.

***

Examining our monotheistic religious traditions — which would necessarily include Judaism, Christianity, and Islam — and comparing them with the Eastern religious traditions born of the Vedas and Upanishads, such as Buddhism or Jainism, we find that they all propose final (certain) answers to the same fundamental questions. How did we get here, i.e., our origin? What *should* we do, i.e., our ethical concerns? What is good, and what should be avoided? Is there a purpose to all of this? What is a worthwhile life? Looking at religion in a strictly positive light, it seems that our innate sense of wonder, curiosity, and the collective force of human intelligence, lie at the heart of all religious doctrines…or of any sincere search for truth.

Given our differing backgrounds, however, it's inevitable that our beliefs will also vary and our paths will diverge in our common search for answers to the fundamental questions of our lives. When I began my own search I believed that Christianity was a religion that was fundamentally different from Buddhism, an opinion I held when I first began studying Buddhism some forty-five years ago. Today I don't believe this to be such a black and white distinction.

Overall my view is more aligned with the psychiatrist turned

THE UNICORN PROBLEM

Existential philosopher Karl Jaspers (1883-1969), who proposed the concept of an "Axial Age" in human history, a turning point for the collective consciousness of humanity: "...the spiritual foundations of humanity were laid simultaneously and independently in China, India, Persia, Judea, and Greece. And these are the foundations upon which humanity still subsists today."

Jaspers maintained that this was a period of awakening for the consciousness of humanity as a whole, a generic wake-up call for the species. It was during this period of renewal that all these cultures eventually abandoned or revised their former convictions and supposed certainties regarding life's fundamental questions and sought deeper insights into the human condition. In this shared quest, Jaspers included the authors of the Upanishads, Lao Tzu, Homer, Socrates, Plato, Parmenides, Heraclitus, Jeremiah, Confucius, and Siddhartha Gautama—among others. It was Jaspers' review of their collective efforts towards the same goals in the same general period of human history that captured my attention, and I began to wonder how much these various traditions shared—how many of their ideas were virtually the same – in their search for final answers to the human experience.

Admittedly, the specific ideas and methods promulgated in these various philosophies and spiritual traditions are oftentimes markedly distinct from each other. For example, most people are aware that Buddhism does not claim a God or Gods as the creator of the Universe, contrary to the major Theist and Deist traditions here in the West. But it does claim an absolute ground of Being, an Ultimate Reality, which, although not identical to the concept of God, is in many ways analogous to our Christian, monotheistic belief in God as a *Necessary and Perfect Being*, as well as Aristotle's definition of God as complete *Actuality*. In addition, Christianity speaks of *salvation* and *resurrection*, whereas Buddhism addresses *liberation* and *reincarnation*. Yet once these concepts are unpacked and we search for the assumptions that have generated the specific conclusions of each religion, their similarities are quite intriguing.

How, we might ask, did the universe come to be if there is no

Creator? After all, don't all things have a cause? Doesn't the chair I am sitting in have a cause, or the fact that I am here at all have a cause? Did all of this, the universe included, simply pop out from nothing? Many of our early Christian Church fathers rejected this possibility as a logical contradiction, in that you cannot reasonably get something from nothing. "From nothing, only nothing" was the maxim.

The ancient pre-Socratic philosophers held the same attitude, attempting to explain all natural events by appealing only to natural causes, these causes themselves dependent upon a common element, such as water or fire. And certainly the philosopher Gottfried Leibniz (1646-1716) likewise rejected this notion of something from nothing when he posited his "Principle of Sufficient Reason" (PSR). For all things, he said, there must be a reason, even as it remains unknown to us for the time being. Hence, the question of our *origins*, or the original cause of both human existence and the existence of the universe in which we find ourselves, and the concomitant issue of human purpose or ends, are the shared concerns of Christian, Buddhist and scientific inquiries alike – concerns, I might add, that become fertile grounds for the Unicorn Problem.

If we think of the monotheistic God as a personality (as do nearly all Theists) with attributes oddly enough much like our own personality traits, we could argue that this bears little to no resemblance to the concept of Buddha Mind in Buddhism, the notion of Brahman or Vishnu in the Vedas, or the Eternal Tao in Taoism. But if we speak of the Judaic or Christian God or Buddha Mind as an Absolute, as philosophers might, or as our human attempt at defining Perfection, in the way that St. Anselm defined God as "that than which nothing greater can be conceived..." then the distinctions between these traditions begin to dissipate.

Many Buddhists would admit that Buddha Mind or Enlightenment is easily conceivable as the epitome of Perfection itself; that there is no state of being more present and complete – more actual – than intrinsic Buddha Nature (Dharmakaya). Indeed, in global summits on world religions it has been suggested that the terms Nirvana, Shunyata, and Dharmakaya fill analogous functions to the concept of God (not, I should add, without strenuous objections). A personal God, the God of traditional Theists, may not actually exist, but the idea of Perfection persists in all religious doctrines, East and West. Thus if we appreciate the Western notion of God from a more abstract than personal position, tilting away from an anthropomorphic rendering, we are better able to understand the position of the 'god-intoxicated philosopher' Baruch Spinoza (1632-1677). He proposed that our minds and bodies are but two attributes of an infinite number of attributes which flow from the same source – God or Nature – take your pick. If this is the case, then once again the differences between Eastern and Western religious traditions enter a gray zone.

Despite these more abstract considerations, the formal doctrine of Christianity does posit God as the creator of all that is and ever will be, whereas Buddhism does not. At this level the doctrines appear hopelessly incompatible. Buddhism does account, however, for the phenomenal realm we loosely call *existence*. How do phenomena—the realm of all appearances – arise at all according to Buddhism? Not from God or the Gods, but, rather, *spontaneously*. This view is substantiated in part by the ancient Vedic idea that all that exists springs from the "golden womb" (Sanskrit: Hiranyagarbha), the intrinsic matrix of the Universe.

Moreover, this Buddhist notion of the spontaneous generation of phenomena – or the Miraculous Display, as it is often called in Vajrayana – is not completely spontaneous after all. In Buddhist metaphysics and ontology, all current events are embedded with events from the past; the "inexorable law of cause and effect" organizes and influences anything we do, think, or feel, resulting in the present moment being the result of all previous moments. This becomes the basis of moral order for Buddhists: from good actions comes only good, from bad only bad consequences. Since Karma is but another name for the causal connections of existence, it stands to reason that the sum of past events have made our current condition inevitable. All that exists may be a spontaneous arising, but there is also an implicit order at work, an overarching determinant quality.

The Buddhist notion of karma is similar to the ancient Greek notion of Fate, (think Oedipus myth), and in particular the Stoics' understanding of destiny (Grk. *moira*). In Stoic philosophy existence is composed of atoms, and this material stuff is impelled strictly through causal relationships. Hence they believed that there was nothing to be done about the way the world runs itself. Reality is a current with which we must swim; a product of a complex history of causal bonds, whose fixed nature is beyond our ability to alter. In our misguided desire to shape the world around us, we struggle in vain against this given nature, unwittingly propagating the ground for our own disillusionment and suffering. For the Stoics:

"…the universe is run according to inexorable law. What happens *must* happen. Therefore, the wise man realizes that to complain is futile and only add to his misery." – *E. Bewkes: Experience, Reason and Faith*

What can be changed, according to both the Stoics and the Buddhists, is our relationship to these given conditions. Destiny or karma predetermines all that exists; all that is, except the mercurial nature of the human will. It seems the human will possesses an inherent freedom that matter cannot duplicate. In this way the realm of human subjectivity remains open-ended, leaving us with the choice of how to respond to the world's demands. And since our subjective realm remains somehow independent of all those karmic debts and fated circumstances, the decisions we make matter. We are, as Jean Paul Sartre (1905-1980) reminds, "…condemned to be free." In this regard, the Stoics advocated the cultivation of *apathia* as the true path to the good life, a life no longer tormented by desires, but rather calmed through the reward of wisdom itself. Buddhists advise a similar route in their practice of *non-attachment* (Sanskrit: the cessation of *upadana*, or clinging). The 14th century mystic Meister Eckhart spoke of the "highest virtue of disinterest." In the 18th century Kant, an extremely amiable and engaging individual, termed this same approach as "disinterestedness."

THE UNICORN PROBLEM

Nonetheless, how the entire Cosmos could be predetermined through the rational principle of causation, and yet we humans remain capable of transcending this fixed law, is not clear for either Buddhists or Stoics. It seems that some notion of free will, intrinsic to human nature alone, would have to be claimed. (In a public lecture, I once heard the Dalai Lama say that Buddhists believe in free will.)

We could also understand the concept of karma outside of the moral domain and link it to a primitive theory of evolution. Theories of evolution after all, date back to the pre-Socratic philosophers (700-500 B.C.E.) within the tradition of natural philosophy. Democritus claimed that all that exists, from chocolate cake to concrete buildings, from creepy cockroaches to crawling human babies, are evolved from the same stuff. "Atoms and the Void," he said, and nothing else. Lucretius (c.99-55 BCE) in his epic work *On The Nature of Things,* describes a sophisticated evolutionary theory in detail. Even the Buddha must have been conversant with the evolutionary theories of his time, concluding that causal relationships were in fact inviolate. That nature indeed evolved wasn't the issue; the real problem to be solved was how this evolutionary process worked, and what the rules of Nature's gambit might be. Karmic law is such a rule.

***

Looking at these philosophical problems from a singularly epistemic lens, we must determine whether truth-bearing propositions about our existence are even possible. Can human perception and understanding, regardless of context, ever perfectly mirror reality itself? Or are we left with the human version only, the true body of Reality always one step beyond our slow-footed minds? As my wife once pointed out, we think we're intelligent because we usually compare ourselves to creatures below us on the evolutionary scale—our pets, for example. Therefore, I can take great pride in believing that I am easily more intelligent than my cat Huxley; as to our other cat, Aldous, I'm not so confident.

These difficulties aside, we discover that in the shared quest for an understanding of our human origins, monotheistic religions, including some Eastern religions, point out the necessity for a *first cause* explanation, or some reason for why there is indeed something rather than nothing. The Judaic, Islamic and Christian theologians called this first cause Yahweh, Allah, or God. In the more esoteric sects this original ground is deemed ineffable, and any proofs of a Creator's existence are dependent on negations, i.e. we can only conceive of what God, Allah, Yahweh or the Buddhist notion of Dharmakaya is not. Centuries earlier, in an attempt to answer the question of why all of nature is in perpetual motion and change, Aristotle referred to this initial instigator of all that exists as the "Unmoved Mover." Imagine a very long row of dominoes, set on end. The "unmoving" finger that pushes that first domino, causing it to tumble into the second domino is the First Cause. Paradoxically, this primary instigator of all motion and change as much draws as pushes things along, like a magnet that attracts metal to its side. Later, theologians such as St. Aquinas, began referring to this Unmoved Mover as a synonym for God.

Below is a variation of what theologians and philosophers refer to as a Cosmological Argument for the necessity of a Creator, an argument based on empirical evidence:

1) Everything that exists has a cause of its existence.

2) The universe exists.

Therefore:

3) The universe has a cause of its existence.

4) If the universe has a cause of its existence, then that cause is God.

Therefore:

5) God exists.

A common refutation (a *defeater* in philosophical circles) is to then ask what caused God, and then the cause of the God that caused the God, and the infinite regress begins. The response to this from both Aristotle and our early theologians was to say that there has to be a beginning to existence, in that we can't simply infer an infinite number of causes – an actual infinity cannot exist. Thus, this First Cause is a *necessary* Being, i.e., God doesn't depend on a cause in order to be; God always is and will be. The philosopher David Hume pointed out that the theologians were unwittingly trapped in a logical fallacy (the Fallacy of Composition): they presumed that since all things *in* the universe have a cause, then the universe itself must have a cause; though possibly true, this is not a logical necessity.

Thus we find that Western monotheist narratives offer us explanations regarding our origin and our fundamental purpose in life; they strive to explain what the good life is all about. They provide us with a mythic – and in that sense, a psychological and moral – perspective on what is Real and True, i.e. what is actually the case. It is through these myths that the story of humanity is recounted. If we are interested in our human origins, how the plot of our human adventure first unfolded, what challenges Fate will inevitably set in our path, and what possible ending may lie in wait for us, these narratives provide us with the answers. We discover that the book of Genesis from the Old Testament might sound like a promising start for humanity, but this very same Judaic myth ends with an apocalypse. Judaic, Christian, and Islamic scriptures inform us of a human chronicle predestined with a definite beginning, middle and end. Ultimately, these religious myths are also referred to as teleo-cosmic dramas, *telos* being the Greek word for purpose or goal. To speak of meaning, such as the meaning of life, is to implicitly posit a purpose to one's existence. And it was believed that there is no meaning (means) without a goal (end or purpose).

In contemporary times, the Existential philosophers refuted this notion of human purpose. They argued that human existence is essentially meaningless, and that there is merely existence itself and our belated attempts at understanding our experiences, wherein we incessantly believe in essences, substances and their ideological offspring, where none actually exist. "Existence precedes essence" is the maxim. Although it may be true that we feel an emotional need to give meaning to our lives and so tell ourselves comforting stories, according to the Existentialists, that meaning is absurd and misleading and in no way intrinsic to our human reality.

Recently published books affirming a "purpose-driven" life as ordained by God have been bestsellers, echoing the sentiments of the early fathers of the Christian Church. We can trace this purpose-driven view of reality back to Aristotle, who claimed that when we ask the *why* of something, such as "Why is the sky blue?" or "Why does water fall from the clouds?" we are actually asking two questions simultaneously: the origin *and* the purpose of that event. If we were to ask why there is life on this planet, we would simultaneously be seeking both its origin and its ultimate purpose. Only when we answer both ends of our query, and answer sufficiently the cause and purpose of an event, do we fully understand it. Happy is the person, said Aristotle, who knows the *cause* of things. Obviously, this can be a tricky enterprise for a scientist, requiring careful examination of the empirical evidence to support any claims, theoretical or otherwise. Religions don't carry this same obligation to sift through the empirical data, since the cause and purpose of life is thought to be already known and fundamentally transcendent, and as such is a revealed Truth as opposed to an empirical fact.

In Aristotle's view, all events actually have four causes, the last of which is their overarching purpose. Things don't just exist; they exist in relationship to their ends or goals. If the question is "Why does rain fall from the clouds?" we could say, "In order to nourish the earth and the sentient beings below." If a sculptor created a statue, that creation is the final cause of his original intent, his *will* if you like; first in time, last in actuality.

Aristotle lists the four causes as:

> The material cause
>
> The formal cause
>
> The efficient cause
>
> The final cause.

All that exists, in his view, is a matter/form synthesis (hylomorphism); there can be no matter without form, and no form without matter. Centuries later Rene Descartes (1596-1650) will echo Aristotle's claim by defining matter as that which occupies space. This synthesis is the substance of everything – the underlying material cause of any object. A contemporary philosophical camp, the *logical positivists* are inclined towards this Aristotelian perspective: reality must be understood within time and space, i.e., matter (or energy) that occupies space (form). According to Aristotle, the Cosmos is sculpted by the original impetus that is concomitantly the final cause. Heavily influenced by Aristotle's philosophy, the early Christians transferred humanity's origin and ultimate purpose to the one and only God.

The notion that nature revealed an inherent order, a design or garden within the jungle of appearances, has been part of the natural philosophical traditions for centuries. This assessment eventually transpired into the Intelligent Design argument of today's religious doctrines. In the monotheistic traditions, design in the universe is offered as proof of a grand Designer – God. God is Aristotle's "final cause" in the grand scheme of things, but for Aristotle this is not so much God as creator of all that exists, but rather the culmination of all potential action into full actuality; God *is* full actuality, i.e. complete. Today, many current quantum theorists reprise Aristotle's concept, referring to the quantum realm as "pure potentiality." As for intelligent design, Hume countered that he would grant design to the universe (after all, the Greeks had spoken of the inherent *Logos* of nature), but whether the designer – or designers – were that intelligent appeared anything but obvious to him. Given the evidence, he said, one could easily draw the opposite conclusion.

Along with their dependence on Aristotle as a means of explicating and bolstering Christian doctrine, the early Church theologians claimed that the true purpose of human existence was to love the Creator – the one true God – eternally, and that achieving union with God fulfills our ultimate purpose here on earth. Buddhism, on the other hand, claims that what *is* always has been, the cyclic episodes of the cosmos spinning endlessly, with no beginning or end, various realms manifesting spontaneously within our fields of awareness. Life's purpose for human beings becomes the cessation of desires and attachments, with the aim of eventually achieving liberation from the perpetual spin of cyclic incarnations.

Thus, in their insistence on a Creator for the Cosmos, our monotheistic traditions require a First Cause, an argument that runs headlong into the wilderness of an infinite regress – definitely Unicorn country. In addition, Bertrand Russell offers an interesting analysis of the cause/effect dichotomy, demonstrating two distinct views of its operations, one from the outside to the inside, and the other from the inside out. For example, the accepted view of causation works from outside to inside: external stimuli cause the mind and nervous system to respond, eventually producing our perceptions, thoughts, feelings, and so on. This is the classic "reductionist" view of reality, wherein all phenomena can be understood as caused by external, material agents, be it God as the First Cause or atomic particles emitted from the Big Bang.

We can, however, flip this perspective, and view the entire process with the human mind or awareness as the basis or ground. How is this accomplished? By realizing that the initial observations and analysis would not be possible without mind or awareness. In other words, the causal agent of mind enables us to know that the material realm even exists. Awareness, in effect, causes matter or energy (external phenomena) to be, and thereby allows us to examine it. Without awareness we could not posit that we abide in a world at all, never mind all this talk of atoms or Boson particles causing everything we know and see. Hence, existence is not the cause of mind, but rather mind is the initial instance of all that exists. The dispute between philosophical Materialists and Idealists seesaws between these two antipodal views.

Putting the problematic nature of causation aside, the major religions, both East and West, supply a defined purpose for their doctrines, an Aristotelian *telos*. This purpose is an absolute goal, as opposed to what are deemed the provisional needs and aspirations that attend our mundane activities. Their belief systems attempt to substantiate, often with cogent arguments, a specific end, be it salvation, rebirth in a pure realm, or simply the right way to live a life – the correct moral view. As mentioned previously, for Christians the goal is to love the Creator with all your heart and thereby achieve salvation, whereas for Buddhism the ultimate goal for any sentient being is to be released from the cycles of re-birth.

It is in this light I would submit that the overarching *telos* of philosophy is Ethics, a normative view of values and an index of virtuous actions that are worthy of human beings. In this way I align myself with Socrates, Plato and, to some extent to Aristotle. The goal or purpose of any philosophical enterprise can be thought of as an attempt to establish a set of values that should be pursued, and to assess how moral or principled we are in our personal and social relationships. In this context, what I found most significant in Sartre's central philosophical work – (nearly one-thousand pages on the nature of Being and Nothingness) – were his views on the moral consequences implied or proposed by the free choices we make.

Ethics is essentially about our relationships, our interactions with other sentient beings, and the intimate connection we have with the environment in which we find ourselves. Ethical problems in philosophy are not addressed in order to justify or repudiate any one moral view, but rather to help us unpack and understand the intents and consequences of our moral perspectives, those very judgments and actions that impact others. This is in large part why compassion is necessarily the vital ingredient in any moral doctrine: human suffering and the necessity of human compassion underlie nearly all moral considerations, including the Greek Ideal of the hero/citizen as exemplified by Socrates. Beyond Thomas Hobbes's (1588-1679) observation that a human life is "solitary, poor, nasty, brutish, and short," moral prescriptions, especially those of Buddhism, insist that without compassion (Sanskrit: *karuna*) there can be no wisdom. Linguist and political theorist Noam Chomsky (1928-) states that[3]

"... In fact, one of the, maybe the most, elementary of moral principles is that of universality, that is, If something's right for me, it's right for you; if it's wrong for you, it's wrong for me. Any moral code that is even worth looking at has that at its core somehow."

***

In the vocabulary of philosophy, the conflicting religious viewpoints mentioned above would be referred to as the metaphysical, ontological, epistemological, and ethical positions of each particular doctrine. All religions and philosophical systems make these kinds of truth-bearing claims about the nature and purpose our human experience. Our metaphysical view and the epistemological constituents that each of us adopts lead directly to our understanding of what necessarily constitutes the good life, the virtuous life, the moral life. When considered collectively these basic categories represent the largest and most encompassing scope of human life we can imagine.

It appears evident that the absolute Truth or Reality sought and described by various religious and mystical doctrines is generic in nature, a common element that runs through all of these diverse narratives. When we examine the ethical standards upheld by the major religions, specifically what each doctrine identifies as virtuous conduct, they differ very little, especially in regard to their intent. Additionally, it is important to note the strong influence of various philosophical systems throughout all of these religious doctrines,

THE UNICORN PROBLEM

especially in reviewing Christian doctrine. Every religion posits a philosophical position, either explicitly or implicitly, i.e. some kind of doctrine. And all religious doctrines make metaphysical, ontological, epistemological, and ethical claims. They then announce, perhaps unfortunately, that these propositions are True—with a capital T.

That is not to suggest that the responses given to these issues are identical in all religions, but rather, to point out that all religions argue over the same mysteries: Where do we come from? How did existence come to be? Do other realities exist? Is there a purpose to all of this? Why do we suffer? Does my individual life really matter? Is death truly the end of our existences? And so on.

In a like fashion, Socrates, Plato and Aristotle, as well as the majority of philosophers that followed, addressed three key issues that relate to all of the questions above:

What is knowledge?
How should I conduct myself?
What is the best form of social governance, i.e. what social system is most just?

And if we can't answer the first question, how can we possibly even begin to address the latter two? This is a defining attribute of the *Unicorn Problem*: How do we justify what we claim to know, our coveted judgments regarding truth and knowledge? Is it by pure reason and demonstrations in logic? Or, could it be that a storehouse of simple beliefs is sufficient for humankind?

For many of us, much of the appeal of Eastern religious doctrines such as those generated from the Upanishads (including Buddhism) derives from their more abstract notion of Ultimate Reality and the Absolute, as well as their strong analytical approach to spiritual realization. In contrast, Christianity appears to be much more dependent on simple belief and faith in order to instantiate its doctrine. Yet when we study the writings of the ancient Christian scholars, we find them to be as much rationalists and philosophers as they are church-going men, more than willing to argue over whether or not faith compels the assent of our will in much the same way that reason compels the assent of our intellect. And let's not forget that Buddhists also speak of faith as the essential ingredient for spiritual progress; as mentioned earlier, most Vajrayana Buddhists refer to this particular form of faith as *Establishing the View*.

Overall, I am inclined to accept the arguments of Jaspers, and agree that the pre-Socratic philosophers, individuals such as Heraclitus, Thales, and Parmenides were indeed walking the path of the Sages. Their goal was that of wisdom (Sophia), and through this very intent they marked the Axial Age of humanity. The Western religious and philosophical traditions are different routes to the same mountaintop sought by the sages of the East, all of them individuals who exemplified the essence of wisdom itself, personalities such as Lao Tzu, Confucius, and Shakyamuni Gautama. They all represent the awakening of the human spirit from its "dogmatic slumber"—the distinguishing attribute of this pivotal turn in human consciousness.

CHAPTER 4
THE HARD PROBLEM

"I will not let anyone walk through my mind with their dirty feet."
Mahatma Gandhi (1869-1948)

"...Suppose I smell roasting coffee beans and say, 'Mmm! Roasting coffee: I love that smell!' Everyone would rightly assume I was talking about my experience. But now suppose my zombie twin produces the same utterance. He, too, seems to be talking about an experience, but in fact he isn't because he's just a zombie. Is he mistaken? Is he lying? Could his utterance somehow be interpreted as true, or is it totally without truth-value?"
Nigel Thomas

ZOMBIES AND UNICORNS LIVING TOGETHER

To be human is simultaneously wondrous and mysterious, made all the more so due to our human consciousness and our ability to be self-aware. Perhaps our existence would be much simpler if we hadn't evolved past the intersection of plants and insects, or if we possessed all of our current abilities except for self-awareness – and, therefore, had no sense of our distinctive separateness, of our individuality and the fate that attends it. The question as 'to what purpose' we are so endowed has not yet been satisfactorily answered. Perhaps it never will be, or perhaps the answer to that question will someday seem unimportant to us.

One thing we do know is that Zombies, those fictional human-like creatures that seem to function exactly as we do – minus that one vital ingredient we call consciousness – would be far more efficient and adaptive than we Homo sapiens. Consciousness, after all, must consume energy (I would argue an inordinate amount of energy), so in principle, at least, creatures identical to us who lack this unique element should also possess superior adaptive skills. Why? Because Zombies would use far less energy than we would in order to accomplish the same task, not being burdened with that pesky attribute of "consciousness." Zombie life, life without a psyche, seems to be so much more practical.

In philosophy our attempts at understanding the true nature of mind or consciousness is dubbed the Hard Problem, coined by the philosopher David Chalmers (1966-). This Hard Problem is immensely difficult for both scientists and philosophers of mind to unravel, for what the actual answers might look like, or more to the point, what questions we should ask initially, including what areas of research we should pursue, seem out of reach. As the contemporary philosopher Patrick Grim of the State University of New York at Stony Brook points out, when we began investigating areas in science that we knew little to nothing about, such as electromagnetism or genetics, at least we knew in what direction to look for the answers. Descriptions of "charges" and "fields" in electricity and "chromosomes" in biology offered us definitions and conceptual hooks that seemed to unlock those realities. To which hooks should we attach our conceptual understandings when investigating "understanding" itself? Currently, the most promising area of research regarding consciousness is in the neurosciences, but whether or not we should be searching for some tiny analog-to-digital exchange unit in the brain – some type of consciousness organ – to explain why we possess consciousness seems more a wish than a reality, or simply the wrong direction to be looking altogether.

For instance, it might in fact be that we receive consciousness more than generate it, i.e., that consciousness is fundamentally non-local. There is the possibility that our brains merely exhibit the effects of consciousness much more so than act as its agent, analogous to a television set that receives signals from afar and then presents to us the images that appear within it. It's hard to imagine that we could dissect a live brain, look deeply inside the engorged tissue, and somehow find a thought, feeling, or perception. According to Socrates and the ancient Greeks, the sense fields may feed us information, but it is necessarily up to the soul to transform this information into knowledge (Some Vedanta philosophies offer a similar explanation). Or, in another direction, perhaps the Tibetan (Vajrayana) Buddhists are correct when they posit the heart as the actual source of human consciousness. It is after all, the first organ to develop in the fetus. Some Buddhist scholars however, claim that that the entire body – not simply the brain or heart – is the basis of the Buddhist understanding of mind. This view would put them to some degree in conformity with Aristotle's description of psyche, or mind.

Or maybe consciousness is the brain as the philosopher Daniel Dennett (1942 -) and the mind-brain identity theorists insist: the mind is the brain in the same way that a rainbow is but light refracting off of water droplets. I can make up stories about pots of gold at rainbow's end, auspicious signs from the heavens above, and whatever else seems appropriate to such a display of natural beauty, but what the rainbow remains is not magical at all, but simply light refracting off of tiny droplets of H2O. I may call this water I am now drinking the nectar of the gods, but still, it is only H2O.

In a similar manner, what we currently call the "mind" is thought by some in the field to be the remnants of folk psychology, the metaphorical way in which we try to explain events we really don't understand. We concoct fanciful stories about disembodied souls, the so-called privileged access each of us has to our private mental life, or the natural lights of reason. But none of these narratives touches on the reality before us: the mind *is* the brain, along with all its purely physical properties. As the MIT professor Marvin Minsky (1927-2015) quipped, "The mind is what the brain does." As for those fanciful stories describing how our mind or soul is radically different from our bodies? Those fairytales are appropriate only for children and the ignorant, and so must be put to rest. In a way, the real message from these MBI theorists is: grow up.

THE UNICORN PROBLEM

Ultimately it may be that the human brain functions primarily as a sophisticated reduction valve. This would mean that the actual purpose of consciousness is to be a traffic cop, only letting pass that information to which we selectively attend. Consciousness serves as a little more than a censor, an inhibitory function that keeps our perceptions and understanding of the world around us tidy, organized, and comfortable. Without the inhibitory process of the brain or consciousness (take your pick), it is possible that we would be so overwhelmed by sensory data that we would all go mad, assuming of course that we haven't done so already.

***

Returning to ancient Greek reflections on the Hard Problem, we can look to Plato's *Phaedo*. In this play reenacting the last days of Socrates' life – the days before he must drink the hemlock as his penalty for not believing in the gods (impiety) and corrupting the youth of Athens with his contemptuous ideas – Socrates reaffirms his fundamentally dualistic view of human nature. We are composed of two essential substances, he suggests, one physical and the other non-material. This non-physical aspect of our being is our "psyche" – the soul or essence of the human animal, the very same essence that in later times would be referred to as *spirit*, *mind*, or even the *élan vital*.

In the *Phaedo,* the character of Socrates presents a number of arguments that support the belief in the soul's immortality. Ultimately Socrates ties his ontological views to his epistemological perspective, employing the soul to support his Theory of Recollection, which states that not all knowledge is sense-driven, and that in fact our important ideas are innate and represent an aspect of the soul. Through the voice of Socrates, Plato argues that our purest and most ideal thoughts, reflections on Truth, Beauty, Justice and so on, could not possibly have arisen from the sense fields. Likewise, the Pythagorean theorem is not knowable through the empirical evidence, nor is the parallel line postulate of Euclid; nor are the concepts of "infinity", "perfection" or "equality" generated through sense impressions. Aside from the knowledge generated by the sense fields, in the view of Socrates, Plato and the centuries of Rationalists that followed, human beings also possess innate knowledge, concepts with which we are born and which we are capable of remembering.

In the *Phaedo* one of the interlocutors states: "...Your favorite doctrine, Socrates, that our learning is simply recollection, if true, also necessarily implies a previous time in which we have learned that which we now recollect. But this would be impossible unless our soul had been somewhere before existing in this form of man; here then is another proof of the soul's immortality."

In this same vignette, Socrates and his friends discuss what might await him once he exits life's stage. Is there indeed life after death? After arguing the various opinions, a few distinct possibilities are decided upon.

> 1) The analogy of a lyre is offered as an explanation of the soul's true nature. Nowhere in the wood body or strings of the lyre is there any hint of a melody waiting to be released, and yet a simple strum of our fingers against those very strings produces something we would never expect: music. Is this the way of the soul as well? Is the soul an epiphenomenon – an "after-effect" – of the physical stuff that constitutes the human body?

> 2) Perhaps the materialists such as Democritus and Leucippus are correct, and when life ends, so does mind or consciousness. The soul for the atomists and the Epicureans that followed was simply a more discrete form of atoms. Atoms and the void compose all that is or ever will be, and the various forms of being are only the offspring of a variety of combinations made from the same building blocks. Hence soul, mind, or consciousness—regardless of which term we prefer – is completely dependent on the body. Why? Because it is produced by physical stuff. If that

is the case, says Socrates, wherein lies the problem with death itself? After all, there will be no one to realize that he or she is actually dead.

3) Or perhaps Pythagoras knows the truth, and the soul or mind is independent of the body, a distinct substance altogether. In this view, the soul would travel to other realms after death and re-enter the cycle of corporeal existence once again. This is referred to as the theory of "transmigration of the soul," and if not identical to Buddhist notions of reincarnation, then it is at least similar enough to give pause. In Buddhism, there are echoes as well of Plato's Theory of Recollection, since the acts of our previous incarnations are reflected in our current life; what we learned (or failed to learn) in our previous life carries over into this one. And if we desire to know about our next life, the Buddha said, simply examine this one closely.

4) It could be that the traditionalists of the time are correct: the soul travels to Hades (one of the original Olympian gods and brother to Zeus) and into the unseen realm of the Underworld. Socrates argues: "... so far as that is concerned, I not only do not grieve, but I have great hopes that there is something in store for the dead... something better for the good than for the wicked."

In Socrates' view, the true philosopher has been training for death all his life, disciplining the passions and appetites of corporeal existence. The ascetic life of the monks and nuns in ancient Christian monasteries was derived from the Greek system of *áskēsis*, i.e. rigorous self-discipline as a spiritual practice, designed for achieving happiness by overcoming worldly desires (Buddhism also claims that we suffer due to our attachment to our desires). A common belief in ancient Greece was that ironically, only death would finally unlock life's secrets, a belief also supported by early Christian doctrine. When we ultimately escape from the imprisonment of our material form and sense fields, all truth and all wisdom will be revealed. We will be purified of the impediments our bodies produce (our karma?).

Socrates goes on to say: "For the soul when on her progress to the world below takes nothing with her but nurture and education; which are indeed said greatly to benefit or greatly to injure the departed, at the very beginning of its pilgrimage in the other world."

As attractive as this acquisition of all truth and wisdom after death might be, a wise person, according to Socrates, would not – unless the circumstances demanded it – deliberately seek his or her own demise. Nevertheless, Socrates advised that mortality was nothing to fear. Why, he asked, should we have trepidations about death if we don't really know what it is? Wouldn't it be mere hubris to speak and act otherwise, implicitly claiming to know what in fact we don't?

In our contemporary scientific community some variation of the first argument presented above – epiphenomenalism – prevails in one form or another. It could be characterized as an offshoot of the old atomistic view of nature. From this perspective, all human activities, including subjective experiences such as thoughts, feelings, imagination, and so forth, are a direct result of physical stuff and its operations. All things are composed of subatomic particles, including us, and this is the only substance within our bodies and against our skin. Consequently our consciousness is also a phenomenon produced by this same physical stuff.

The Spanish-American philosopher George Santayana (1863-1952), who was an adherent of this view, offered the analogy of a candle. If we were to examine a candle, analyze its composition, the wax and the wick embedded within it, we would have no reason to suspect its capacity to produce heat and light. There is no heat or light in the wax, nor in the wick. Yet in actuality this candle does indeed produce something radically different from what any of its constituents would lead us to believe. Thus, though we might examine any of our own body's physical stuff to the nth degree, nowhere would we discover a luminous consciousness – yet there it is, an apparent outcome of that very material.

THE UNICORN PROBLEM

If this is the case, then it necessarily follows that if we take away the wax or the wick of the candle, or the wood and metal of the lyre, there would be no epiphenomena, no separate after-the-fact phenomena such as light or music. Without the physical stuff, there is no fire to illuminate our night, no music to fill our dancehalls. So wouldn't the case be the same with consciousness or the soul? No physical matter... no mind? No physical stuff, no soul or psyche apart from it?

In our modern view of cognitive neurophysiology and medicine, once the brain is dead, consciousness necessarily dies with it. Most neuroscientists do not seriously entertain the notion of some intangible substance distinct from matter. Physical stuff is all we have, and when it goes we all go — atoms and the void, and nothing in between. Not a very comforting picture, but consistent with the modern physicalist view of the human condition.

This is where we might say that the religious or mythic view of our human condition gains the upper hand on science. Science is like the weather and the impartial forces of nature: it either rains, or shines, and we are subject to its callous fickleness. It makes no difference if the Dalai Lama or I fall over the edge of a cliff: we are both subject to the same law of gravity. Science is not interested in our personal feelings about the truth of Newton's theory of gravity. It is only interested in employing the theory — *truth is what works,* as pragmatists would say — and if errors show up down the way, they are to be corrected. Actually these corrections are welcomed since they bring us ever closer to the Truth. Our Western religious traditions, on the other hand, contend that our relationship with the Divine (whatever or whoever that might be) is deeply personal. We establish an intimate, pacifying relationship with the Divine. As Sigmund Freud (1856-1939) pointed out, religions provide us with a sense of safety and comfort in the midst of a dangerous world.

Contrarily, if a person of faith loses that faith and begins to question the truth of God's existence or her or his relationship with the Divine, this is a very big deal. A crisis of faith can be seriously debilitating, both emotionally and psychologically. Thus religion requires an emotional engagement from us, whereas science is essentially dispassionate and seeks to eliminate any personal component in its explanations; it is "objective," and essentially abstract in nature, rather than particular or concrete, as personal events tend to be. Scientists don't seek emotional solace through their study of nature. Instead they seek laws that apply to everyone at all times – whether we like them or not.

***

At this point it would be helpful consider the nature of science: is it merely a body of knowledge? If so, how was that body brought to life? Most of us know that science is foremost a method of collecting knowledge, a conceptual net that necessarily excludes much if not most of our everyday experiences. In addition science has obviously adopted the dispassionate outlook that signifies the philosophical view of matters. After all, what is a scientific view if not objective in nature? But what is the overall methodology and how was it developed?

There have been two primary approaches to establishing the modern empirical method of scientific inquiry. One embraces the subjective realm, those experiences granted to us through the privileged access of our psyches. If we grant that our mental realm is self-evident, independent of the dubious nature of sense experiences, we may follow up this realization with an endless number of deductions. Why is that? Because we have established a universal Truth about which it would be impossible to be wrong. If we then proceed from this universal Truth with sound reasoning, the storehouse of knowledge is opened wide. We obtain Truth that is timeless, universal, necessary and certain.

This was the view of Rene Descartes – scientist, swordsman, recluse, mathematician and most significantly, a rationalist in the lineage of Socrates and Plato. In his *Meditations* he resolved to doubt everything he believed. He was willing to admit that perhaps everything he thought was true was in fact false; fire isn't hot, and the

THE UNICORN PROBLEM

physical world is but a dream. Does there exist, he wondered, anything beyond all doubt, something so certain that it must be accepted as a brute fact? His answer came through his *Cogito Argument*, in which he claims to have succeeded in his introspective quest. I have loosely translated his argument in syllogistic form below.

If I doubt that I exist, then there must be a doubter. Therefore, I must exist.
If I think, then there must be a thinker. Therefore, I must be a "thinking thing".
I must, therefore, be. This is also certain. This is a "clear and distinct idea" about which it is impossible to be wrong. It is certain.

For Descartes this knowledge of being a doubting, thinking thing is *foundational*. Although he does conclude that what is doing the thinking is some kind of ambiguous "thing," he is not actually making an ontological claim. Rather he is making an epistemological claim and believes that he has now established certain knowledge, knowledge that is beyond all doubt, a truth-claim about which it is impossible to be wrong. The overall knowledge problem has been solved, and all thoughts of Unicorns have been forever banished. Even if the external world is naught but a dream, the dreamer must *be*. For Descartes, objective experience was the problem, and the mind was the solution. All inquiries regarding truth and knowledge required a base from which to begin, an axiomatic clear and distinct idea as a reliable footing, or all of what we deem factual – the entire body of evidence that we carefully collect – could easily free-fall from its faulty premises into misleading and erroneous conclusions.

The second approach to the scientific method is that of Francis Bacon (1561-1626). For Bacon the human mind was not the solution, as it was with Descartes – it was actually the obstacle in our quest for Truth. The mind – or more specifically, the way in which we employ the mind's faculties – is the root of the epistemological problems in science and philosophy. It's why all those brightly colored Unicorns keep popping up.

MITCHELL J. FRANGADAKIS

Forget the immutable and eternal laws sought by ancient natural philosophers and theologians. Be led instead by the evidence provided by nature herself. Collect data. Share it with others seeking knowledge in the same way. The scientific mind must be trained to make observations objectively, in an unbiased fashion, following no preconceived doctrine (as there must be within the Church and its revealed Truth), or any philosophical preconceptions as to what is real and true. The mind must rid itself of its "idols," those mental icons that represent deep-rooted systems of belief and cognitive bias.

Bacon listed the following:

1) Idols of the Tribe (*Idola tribus*): This denotes humanity's tendency to perceive more order and regularity in systems than is actually present, and is due to people investing their own preconceived opinions or imaginary qualities in what they observe.

2) Idols of the Cave (*Idola specus*): This denotes the tendency of individuals to perceive and interpret everything through the lens of their own particular interests and outlook.

3) Idols of the Marketplace (*Idola fori*): This denotes the confusion arising from misuse or misunderstanding in the expression of words and ideas.

4) Idols of the Theatre (*Idola theatri*): This denotes the tendency to accept any long-standing academically-presented dogma as an article of truth without question.

For Bacon, this was the correct approach to the scientific method: accept the necessity of inductive reasoning. The scientist must be trained to collect bits of data and to eventually generate a hypothesis from that data – not the other way around. Don't start with some grand scheme – a magisterium – accepting it as self-evidently true, and then go about deducing certain conclusions. If I accept fundamental principles or facts as true – true in a way that

THE UNICORN PROBLEM

requires no further justification – then almost anything can follow, from the necessary truth of God's existence to "factual" stories about Unicorns.

Get rid of the cognitive biases; down with traditional approaches to knowledge; read the book of nature from Nature herself, and leave the Bible or any other revealed scriptures to others. Learn what it means to be objective in your explanations, and build up humanity's body of truth and knowledge slowly, each generation adding new elements to the Big Picture until ultimately Reality will stand naked before us. And by the way, geniuses like Rene Descartes need not apply. Science needs researchers, data collectors, people who are willing to spend a lifetime studying one small piece of the puzzle, individuals who are more than happy working in the tradition of Aristotle and his laborious studies of the mating habits of cuttlefish.

Francis Bacon was a lawyer and political player more so than a philosopher or scientist, and it could be argued, was not a metaphysician. But he was intrigued by geometric problems in mathematics and he did believe in the application of objective, empirical observations when unraveling Nature's secrets; Nature was the teacher, and we but her humble students. His contribution to the scientific method is undeniable and of unquestionable value.

This is the rudimentary background of the scientific approach to truth and reality. Historically, there have been two opposing undercurrents, one in the direction of *Plato's Gods* (such as Descartes followed) and, in the other direction, the *Earth Giants* – followed by Bacon. These crosscurrents within scientific epistemology, one side running on pure reason and the other primarily on empirical evidence, are what Dr. Steven Goldman (1941-) refers to as the *Science Wars*. Plato's war between the Gods and Earth Giants, described some two millennia ago, lives on to fight another day.

Of course, instead of a disjunctive either/or proposition, it may be the case that both the Gods and the Earth Giants are correct, at least in a limited sense. In principle, it is possible that we will come to know all there is to know about the human experience – its cause and even its ultimate purpose, if there be any – while at the same time remaining grossly ignorant of Reality at large. At some time in the far future our human realm might be entirely mapped, while we necessarily remain surrounded by a vast unknown. We will be like Plato's Gods because our knowledge of human reality, for all intents and purposes, will be complete at last. At the same time we will have to remain resigned to the fact that the Reality of the universe – though present – remains obfuscated by our limited human perspectives, and the Earth Giants are once again affirmed.

When examining the scientific method, we should keep in mind that modern science admits only measurements of time and space into the knowledge game (It is interesting to note that one of the translations of the Sanskrit word for "illusion" – *maya* – can be defined as: "to measure"). If we ask *why* something happened, what the reasons were for the event occurring, then we are in effect requesting the cause of the matter at hand. In the scientific method, all explanations of Nature's display must be founded on natural causes. When a scientist explains why the planetary bodies move in the way they do, any appeal to gods, gnomes, or the hand of the Creator himself as an explanation is deemed an invalid hypothesis. All explanations must occur solely within time and space, a necessarily nature-based orientation.

Needless to say, most religions have a problem with this particular taboo, oftentimes feeling left out of the serious conversations regarding knowledge and truth. The very nature of scientific inquiry, this requirement that all reasons for natural events be grounded in nature alone, leaves religious judgments that rely on supernatural explanations out of the conversation. Ironically, this absence of any need for a supernatural explanation of human events is what makes science such an impersonal process. It does not buttress what our experience tells us. For instance, if I touch the cup on my table, its surface feels cool and hard. Science countermands this experience, explaining that the cup is mostly empty space, and that the stuff that comprises that cup is neither hot nor cold. My personal experience of phenomena and the scientific explanation of the actual cause of my phenomena seemed to occur, regardless of the original intent, in two distinct realms.

Since physicists treat the human mind as yet another swirling mixture of atoms and the void, not different in that respect from any other physical object that occupies space and takes up time, a general truth-bearing claim of science is that all experiences are reducible to physics – the overall "reductionist" view of reality. And though science may explain the whole range of events in our lives in terms of the properties of matter and energy, when I touch the hot stove, I don't experience it as a collection of atoms bombarding my skin. Instead, I feel pain. We experience the truth of physics not as a physical, objective fact, but rather as a feeling or value. In philosophy, this internal experience is termed a *quale* or *qualia* (as opposed to a quantum or quanta), or as the philosopher Dennett put it: "an unfamiliar term for something that could not be more familiar to each of us: the ways things seem to us." No quantity of things can ever add up to the *quality* of an experience, that of which we feel, think, and speak.

The ontological issue, and a critical aspect in our attempts to understand human cognition, is this: how does the physical stuff of the supposed real world, which produces responses in our physical bodies, then end up causing something that doesn't seem physical at all: subjective experiences and consciousness? Is this a physical problem to solve, as in the current research in cognitive neuroscience that hopes to solve the Hard Problem of Consciousness, or is the problem essentially metaphysical? The central consideration here is the relationship between personal experience and an impersonal Reality that should remain constant regardless of who's looking at it. If you say it's cold and I say it's hot, even though our personal experiences contradict one another, we assume that we are drawing different conclusions from one and the same Reality. Reality is something like what the entertainer Jimmy Durante (1893-1980) used to say as he looked up into the fading spotlight at the end of his T.V. show: "It's bigger than the both of us!"

Thus, we are left to wonder: *Is consciousness a unique substance unto itself?*

In the dualistic view of Reality, mind and body are two distinct substances, similar to the arguments we heard from Socrates and, centuries later, from Descartes. And if pressed for an explanation, this is probably the view most of us would propose: it is, after all, common sense. What could be more obvious then the public realm of time and space, that realm of being that every physical form, including our bodies, occupies? Our mental life feels totally private, whereas our bodies are on display for anyone who bothers to look. Isn't this corporeal realm obviously distinct from the formless realm we call "subjectivity?" How tall is a thought? If we weigh our bodies and stare in dumb disbelief at the numbers that pop up on the scale, how much does that disbelief weigh? Aren't we left with two radically different realms of experience, one outside and the other within – one measurable, and the other simple feeling or qualia?

From the Buddhist perspective, this dualistic nature of our experiences arises from a single source, a metaphysical view similar to that of Spinoza. The subjective feelings (the *qualia*) comprise one mode, but these subjective experiences require a content of some sort. It could be any object of consciousness, regardless of whether it is my perception of the pen on the table, my memory of yesterday's dramas, or the dream I had this morning. This side we could call physical. It doesn't really matter, just so we distinguish it from the distinct experience of solitary awareness, consciousness or mind absent of specific content.

Lama Zopa from the Tibetan Buddhist lineage states: "What is the mind? It is a phenomenon that is not body, not substantial, has no form, no shape, no color, but, like a mirror, can clearly reflect objects."

Contrarily, normal consciousness always possesses content. But the Pure Awareness referred to in Buddhist texts is singularly void of content (other than its own adamantine quality); it is radically self-sufficient, a sense of knowing without needing to know anything in particular, much like the attributes of the Theists' God. This mode

THE UNICORN PROBLEM

of awareness is void of mental, physical, or emotional entanglements – beyond all hope or fear and divorced from the all objects of discrimination. Pure Awareness (Tibetan: *Rigpa*) ultimately rests in its own nature, and it is not open to any personal ownership. In this way, its attributes are radically different from normal consciousness, or what we normally refer to as mental or cognitive experiences and concepts. The Buddhist claim is that Rigpa is our essential nature and reveals itself once the veils of ignorance have been lifted from our psyches. This view invites the question: why do I search for that which I already possess? Vajrayana Buddhism also claims that once we have generated this kind of cognitive clarity, i.e., once we have established *The View*, our psychic health is restored. Why is this? Because we will have realized that that all phenomena, including our own consciousness, have always been deities in disguise.

If we adopt the Buddhist view of mind we are forced to redefine subjectivity itself; it is not simply the normal monkey-mind of human consciousness, jumping and clutching from one branch of thought, imagination, memory and perception to another. Rigpa is a conscious state of equanimity, a sense of internal harmony and balance and, if one is fortunate enough, is capable of producing the subjective experience of pure bliss. Although these two attributes of mind appear to be different – mind with an object and mind without an object – in the Non-Dual (Sanskrit: Advaita) philosophy of Buddhism, they are, paradoxically, one and the same. The yin-yang nature of any feeling, thought or perception – the object and the subject for whom this experience is occurring – can be mentally discriminated into various attributes, but from the Non-dual view they have always comprised a singular Reality, differing aspects of the same continuum. In this sense, the Dzogchen or Non-dual view of Vajrayana Buddhism redeems the sense fields, insisting that there really is no self and other, no inside and outside, no subjective/objective, mind/body split. The ground of Pure Awareness, the essential nature of our minds, and the content that appears within it, are necessarily blended into one nature, or, as is often stipulated, of "one taste."

For Socrates and Plato the psyche (mind or soul) was immortal, due in large part to its simplicity, yet another attribute Theists ascribe to their God. Simplicity, in this instance, means the absence of any parts…nothing to come together or fall apart. No elements involved, no matter dissolving or spiraling back into the void. That which does not depend on anything outside of itself cannot therefore decline. Time and space are irrelevant since the soul does not consist of any stuff. Again, from the scientific perspective this is literally a nonsensical proposition.

As already noted, for philosophers such as Socrates the soul was essential to our ability to think, feel, and perceive. The soul was the seat or ground of these functions, and in that sense the true self of any human being. Socrates' Theory of Recollection, which claimed that human beings possess innate ideas (Pure Forms), required souls that were able to transfer this natural wisdom from one lifetime to the next. However problematic this description may be, the soul remained the essence of human existence, the primary ingredient without which we could not be what we are. A strong claim can be made that many of the ancient Greek philosophers believed the soul to be essential, immortal, as well as the eternal Knower within us.

According to this point of view, when I refer to my self, I am referring to a non-material substance, my soul or psyche. My attributes may change over time, but who I am in essence remains constant. It is as if the soul is an always innocent and incorruptible child, whereas our bodies slowly wither under the disturbing influences of our earthly conditions.

"… the philosopher more than other men frees the soul from association with the body as much as possible. Body and soul are Separate, then. The philosopher frees himself from the body because the body is an impediment to the attainment of truth". —*Plato's Phaedo*

Overall, the concept of the *soul* or *psyche* has a fascinating history. Most of us are familiar with the use of this term from the word *psychology*, which we take to mean the study of the psyche or mind. As we can see from Plato and his dialogs, its original connotation was that of an independent substance, radically different from any material or corporeal substance. Descartes made this concept the cornerstone of his ontology, the inherent dualism of mind and body, what we today call *Cartesian Dualism*. As noted earlier, the word *psyche* originally meant not mind, but rather soul. Who thinks? Who feels? Who perceives? The soul. What gives us the power to reason, our "natural lights" as Descartes would call it? The soul. In this wise, the soul becomes the essence of who we are as human beings, i.e. that without which we could not be the sentient beings that we are. The soul is not so much merely the "witness" as sometimes described in translations of Eastern religious scriptures, but is perhaps better described as *that which knows or illuminates*.

Buddhist doctrine exemplifies this view: "Mind is not an entity or 'thing,' so there is nothing that is actually an agent giving rise to anything. The word, 'mind' is simply a term mentally labeled onto the occurrence of the subjective event of the giving rise to something." – Dr. A. Berzin, *Mahamudra*

For theologians such as St. Augustine, St. Anselm and St. Aquinas, the meaning of soul began to shift from the ancient Greek understanding. No doubt the persistent sentiment that somehow our true nature is entrapped in a physical form – with all of its assets and liabilities – remained. It was assumed we were all prisoners in Plato's Cave, captive either through the inherent commands of necessities and needs, the natural ignorance of homo sapiens, or in Christian doctrine, our sins inherited from humanity's fall from grace.

St. Anselm eventually shifted the meaning of *psyche* to something more in the manner that we might speak of *mind* today. In philosophy we say that we have *privileged access* to our subjective experiences, i.e. our mental lives. Paranormal psychology aside, no one else is privy to our personal experiences. The word *psyche* was soon enough translated into Latin as *anima* or *animus*, that which animated the physical body, similar to the élan vital of Henri Bergson

(1859-1941) centuries later. Spirit (spiritus), mind (mens) and reason (ratio) eventually took on equivalent meanings.

In summation, the Saints explained the soul's nature in this way:
> The purpose of human life is to love God;
>
> God would not will this love to cease;
>
> Therefore, the soul is immortal.

Now the soul had received its true purpose, for as Aristotle reminded, we cannot know a thing fully unless we understand its goal, i.e. the final cause.

Today most of us would shrug our shoulders and call the mind, soul, spirit (or whatever), exactly what we believe it to be: the brain. I would assume that the most sought-after grants in today's "psyche-logy" doctoral programs are directly related to the neurosciences. Everyone is busily trying to construct a road map though the gray matter – a map, not unlike those maps discovered in adventure stories that inevitably point toward gold. We will finally reveal how our deepest thoughts and emotions are nothing more than positive and negative discharges of neurotransmitters and the circuits through which they prefer to gallop.

As mentioned earlier, most of the current views of human cognition are essentially reductionist in nature. This means than any mental experience can be reduced to a biological process, which itself depends on molecular exchanges at the chemical level, and the chemical interactions are necessarily reducible to electron shifts at the atomic level. In the end – unless we accept some emergent properties for each level of the continuum – everything tumbles down to quantum mechanics, the subatomic level, and how anti-matter is somehow matter in disguise. Overall, the laws of physics run the whole show.

In response to this reductionist view, Nagel presents the following thought experiment: "I assume we all believe that bats have

THE UNICORN PROBLEM

experience. After all, they are mammals, and there is no more doubt they have experience than mice or whales have experience...

"We know that bats perceive the external world primarily by sonar, detecting the reflections from objects generated by their own high frequency shrieks. Their brains are designed to correlate the outgoing impulses with the subsequent echoes, and this information allows the bat to make precise discriminations comparable to those we make by vision.

"But I want to know what it is like *for a bat to be a bat.*"

We find that Nagel's thought experiment refutes a strictly physical view of reality, for it seems that the physical stuff of a sentient being must be radically distinct from the actual experience of being something physical. Physical stuff happens outside, and experience remains strictly internal. Nagel's experiment also questions the long-standing belief that subjectivity is but our memories at work. Some have claimed that to have an experience of being something is to remember what that experience is like. Memory is who and what we are. Locke based his theory of self-identity on this premise. In his thought experiment, he proposed that if a Prince were to wake up one fine morning inside a cobbler's body and the cobbler awakened inside the Prince's body, they would both be very confused. Why? Because the key to their knowledge of who they are resides in their conscious memory, activated upon awakening. Once alert, each would realize their true identity, despite the radical switch in physical forms. In other words, the cobbler would be the same cobbler to everyone but himself, and the same goes for the Prince. This was Locke's counterpoint to the belief that self-identity is fundamentally based on our physical bodies alone, and to the speculations that posited an amorphous soul as the essence of our self-identity.

If we consider Descartes' claim that subjectivity is indubitable, and also accept Nagel's argument that our subjective experiences remain radically different from any physical components we might describe, we have returned to the same dualistic view considered in Plato's *Phaedo*: Reality is composed of two distinct substances, one physical and the other mental, one of the body and the other of the soul.

John Dewey (1861-1947) attempted to unify this mind/body split by pointing out what appears most obvious: the body and the mind are *of* experience, not *in* experience. This is so in the same way that a mountain is of the world, not in the world. Hence, we could speculate that what is out there as an objective reality and what we know and feel that reality to be – the quality of our experiences – is derived from the same source: simple experience, bereft of any assumptions. Although Dewey would not argue that God, Buddha Mind, or even the psyche is the overarching reality that creates human experience, in effect he split the difference between the Gods who live in the realm of Pure Ideas, and the Earth Giants who ground their philosophy in a strict form of materialism. According to both Dewey and Buddhists, both sides of this philosophical struggle subsist within the same house.

Given the subtlety and complexity of the human mind attempting to investigate itself, and despite the various definitions given in the numerous philosophical systems of the East, I would suggest that the common word, *consciousness,* be employed as a bridge between the Eastern and Western schools of thought. This concept best describes what the Hard Problem of Mind in Western philosophy means, and rather than speak of mind, we are better served if we consider consciousness to be the nut that needs cracking. Perhaps it is a better English term for the Buddhist meaning of *citta*, as well, a Sanskrit term commonly translated as *mind*. Determining appropriate terms for these subjective experiences is difficult, especially if we want to discriminate between various states of consciousness, such as attentiveness, intention, perception, self-awareness, memory, or even the nature of pure feeling…be it pleasure, pain, or indifference. We should also consider that we "know" (whatever that term might ultimately mean) that we are conscious, and thus recognize that awareness is antecedent to conscious states, those mental functions of our normal waking experiences. All of this lends credence to the Buddhist notion that awareness is, indeed, primordial.

Dudjom Lingpa (1835-1904), a Terton (Treasure Holder) in the Tibetan Buddhist tradition admonishes: "Not knowing how to distinguish between mind and awareness, you mistake mind for awareness, which is a fault in that it becomes a cause that impedes your progress to the ground of liberation. Therefore, distinguish between them!"

Which of these categories should we be attending to if we are serious about solving the Hard Problem of human consciousness? Overall, it seems that the knowledge, understanding and illumination that consciousness, mind or awareness produces appears to be both a gift and a burden for humankind.

***

Regardless of the subject being addressed, be it the mystery of consciousness or the practical matters of living a good life, one substantial rift between religious doctrines and the practice of philosophy is this: religions produce final answers to the questions we have been asking, answers that are claimed as True with a capital T, whereas philosophy, even though it also seeks the big Truth, places equal if not more emphasis on the questions we ask rather than the answers we provide. We could say that the shape of the questions asked determines or restricts the answers we discover. A student once dropped a poster in my mailbox that read:

> Religion: Answers that cannot be questioned.
> Philosophy: Questions that may never be answered.

The answers in religion regarding Ultimate Reality are thought to be a complete product. Philosophers' answers remain suspect always, even if logically defended and presented with complete sincerity and conviction. Philosophers are no less skeptical of philosophical doctrines than are most people when asked to believe what their politicians tell them. Furthermore, before positing any answer at all, a good philosopher wonders: Am I asking the right question? Are these the questions appropriate for the issue at hand? And once the most efficient or elegant question has been posed, the philosophical process demands that we begin with as few presuppositions as possible. In philosophy the process of criticism is perpetually active: if absolute solutions are proposed, they are immediately subject to peer review, the attendant result being that the philosophical quest for timeless, universal, necessary and certain Truth has, to this point, remained on hold.

It is claimed that this absence of presuppositions is the very value of logic in the philosophical inquiry. Logic is (by definition) a neutral method, devoid of personal values and absent the biases most of us bring into our experiences. Logic serves as an exercise in pure abstraction and the realm of possible truths, wherein concrete, individual examples are incidental, and any specific content can be plugged into its generic definitions, formulas and regulations. Hence the thinking goes that logic interjects no unintentional prejudice into the questions under consideration. Logicians, like mathematicians, claim their measurement systems in no way alter the reality of the event being examined. Logic is assumed to be value-neutral, and according to Bertrand Russell and others, mathematics is grounded in logic. This was the predominant view of many natural philosophers and is still a prevalent view among scientists today. Reason is capable of objectivity in the purest sense of that word, especially rational thought translated into pure mathematics.

When an archaeologist, for example, uncovers an ancient vase and describes it in detail, alluding to its color, design, composition and time period, it seems obvious that he or she is engaged in an objective procedure, simply describing what has been revealed from beneath the earth. The archaeologist's analysis of the vase in no way alters its original design, color, form, or origin. Now the question is: does *reason* have this same descriptive characteristic, or does it impart its own bias onto that which it describes? Does reason or logic truly describe the reality that has been unearthed, or is it just another

THE UNICORN PROBLEM

human faculty, subject to the same distortions that we find with our sense perceptions? When the 20th century post-modern critique of science and philosophy was in full swing, logic was deemed but another example of a socially constructed reality, anything but impersonal and objective in nature.

Let's imagine, as the philosopher Daniel N. Robinson (1937-) suggests, a solitary mathematician struggling with a purely theoretical problem. She is developing her mathematical equations without any practical applications in mind. One night the final proof comes to her in a dream. Ultimately, her solution is published. No one can find any use for her proof, but it makes for interesting speculation. The mathematical formulas she has developed follow in the Platonic tradition by being both elegant (beautiful) and simple. Then let's say that 100 years later, another scientist is struggling to find a mathematical formula that explains turbulence in gases. He fortuitously stumbles upon this same presumed useless mathematical formula that was generated 100 years prior. To his surprise and delight, he finds that it solves his problem perfectly! How is it that these mind-made symbols within mathematics can accurately describe a natural process, especially when that natural process is not even the object of observation and study? It is precisely this uncanny correspondence between pure reason and actual phenomena that leads most rationalists to believe that nature, despite appearances, is inherently logical.

It appears that nature taunts us with her riddles and humanity responds, as would the gods, with "consummate perspicacity," knocking down one impediment to knowledge after another. For centuries mathematicians struggled with the problem of squaring the cube, but eventually Descartes – in his writings for the secretive and mysterious Rosicrucian society – solved what seemed to be the unsolvable. Perhaps the medieval theologians were onto something with their ontological notion of the Great Chain of Being, with humanity situated somewhere between beasts and angels. Perhaps our station in life is situated such that we are offered a glimpse of these higher realms…or even Reality itself?

MITCHELL J. FRANGADAKIS

How do the Earth Giants respond to claims of timeless and universal Truth? Who is it, they might ask, who is capable of jumping outside of mind and body in order to inspect what Reality truly is? All we possess is human form, and all of our attempts to make sense of what we think, feel, and perceive can never circumvent the limits of our human condition. We are all tightly bound to our egocentric world-view. We don't experience reality, per se; rather, we have experiences only, some of which we claim to be real, and others not. Any claims about Reality, about what lies beyond our discursive thoughts, feeling, and perceptions, is mere speculation, sometimes true, but only true in the most ordinary and practical sense...a human truth and nothing more.

There is a somewhat novel branch in the theories of knowledge called evolutionary epistemology. This branch maintains that since human beings are part of an evolutionary process, our reason and language development are necessarily part of this evolution. As such, our rational faculties are adaptive and beneficial. Additionally, since reason is a natural development that must serve an adaptive function, human beings are capable of understanding their world while at the same time remaining a participant in that world, one member species among billions on planet earth. Similar to Dewey's stance, our conceptual descriptions of the universe and ourselves are of the Earth and the Gods simultaneously. In this way it is thought that reason is more than capable of providing the insights and understanding we require for living the good life as human beings.

Despite the emphasis in contemporary philosophy on the analytic approach, which includes the analysis of language itself, there is a history of systematic philosophers who have attempted to answer all the questions that philosophers, as well as religious adepts, have pondered over the centuries, answers regarding human origins, purpose, knowledge, and so forth. Plato is the one who originally set the table, preparing the banquet that philosophers such as Locke, Descartes, Leibniz, Spinoza, Hegel and others in our Western tradition feasted upon throughout their lives. The natural philosopher

THE UNICORN PROBLEM

Alfred North Whitehead (1861-1947) — one of the few scientists who reviewed and actually understood Einstein's Theory of General Relativity before it was released for public viewing — claimed that all of philosophy to date is but a footnote to Plato. And here is a short list of 'Plato's Menu':

> What is Ultimate Reality? (Metaphysics)
>
> What is human nature? (Ontology/Psychology)
>
> How should we conduct ourselves? (Ethics/Moral Systems)
>
> What does it mean to know something?
>
> (Epistemology /Mathematics/Logic)
>
> Is there a right way of forming social institutions?(Political
>
> Science/Education/Sociology
>
> And finally: What is the Good Life? Or put in more personal terms: *How can I be happy?*

Which invites yet another question: What is the right way to live? Are there factual, undeniable truths "out there" to guide all of us in making this determination, or is this up to our personal judgment alone? And, if it is entirely for each of us to mold our lives, then how do we determine what's actually true and what's false? Does it even matter if it's true or false, if indeed it is my own free choice to believe one way or the other? These were the types of questions that intrigued Socrates and his students, Plato and Aristotle.

I would suggest that we draw conclusions about a 'good' life or the right way to live by our understanding our own existence, including the nature of human consciousness. For instance, we could start by asking ourselves how often we consciously strive to live what we understand to be the good life. Do we even know what the "good life" is supposed to be? We could also ask ourselves how often we consciously examine the choices we make between wrong and right, between truth and falsehood, good and bad, reality and illusion. Consciously thinking through the decisions we make in life is one way we might conform to the essential meaning of the Good, the in-and-of-itself kind of final Good that Socrates sought.

I would agree with Aristotle, who stated that the Good for humanity, that very same Good that, though not identical, comports with the transcendent Good of Plato, is a flourishing life, a growth that springs from within and fulfills us, a developmental maturation that unfolds our potential into actuality. And, as already mentioned, Aristotle's God was *full Actuality*. Just as all physical bodies mature, our soul (which for Aristotle was synonymous with our biological nature) matures by fully actualizing its innate capacities, and in this way completes its mission. We could say that Aristotle brings the Pure Ideals of Plato back into the realm of matter and physical forms, our hearts and minds included.

Throughout the centuries, from the time of Plato to the present day, philosophers, scientists, and religious adepts have taken some or all of these questions quite seriously, each fulfilling in his or her own way the promise of an examined life. Socrates set a worthy example with the example of his own life, absorbed in a quest for truth and knowledge, constantly questioning and evaluating his own beliefs and intentions for their meaning, moral value, and ethical worth. He taught that to have a happy life, a truly prosperous life, we must examine and understand our deepest intentions and accept full responsibility for the way in which we live our lives. It is in this manner that our conscious nature reveals itself, priming the path to self-mastery.

CHAPTER 5
FAITH AND REALITY

"It is man's natural sickness to believe that he possesses the truth."
Blaise Pascal

In an encyclical letter Pope John Paul II wrote: "Faith and reason are like two wings on which the human spirit rises to the contemplation of truth; and God has placed in the human heart a desire to know the truth–in a word, to know himself – so that, by knowing and loving God, men and women may also come to the fullness of truth about themselves."

OUR BELIEF IN UNICORNS

The fundamental antipathy between religion and most philosophical traditions lies in the presumed conflict between faith and reason. If religion is our guide, then we are directed both by its belief system and the faith it engenders, whereas philosophy invests its trust in reason and critical analysis, dubious of any truth based on faith alone. Hence we arrive at the faith/reason controversy that interjects itself into most dialogs between religious and philosophical traditions.

The Christian Monk Tertullian (160-225 CE) responded to the faith/reason controversy by asking his own question: What does Athens (reason) have to do with Jerusalem (faith)? We have already defined reason as that which compels the assent of our intellect. But what should we make of faith? Although there is no agreed upon exegesis, it can be said to be a form of fidelity or personal commitment to a particular way of governing our lives.

Here are a few models of faith according to the Stanford Encyclopedia of Philosophy:

> The 'Purely Affective' model: This is faith as a feeling of existential confidence. We find this kind of faith in the Sufi Tradition, as well as in the Buddhist notion of establishing confidence in "The View."

> The 'Special Knowledge' model: This means faith as knowledge of specific truths, revealed by God. The "welcome of certainty" is an example of the special knowledge model of faith found in the writing of the Persian mystic Al-Ghazali (1058-1111 CE).

> The 'Doxastic Venture' model: Faith is now the sole criterion to one's belief that God exists, beyond the need for evidence and independent of reason. This form of faith echoes the tenets of Fideism and exemplifies the current fundamentalist movement in Christian America.

Contrary to these models, philosophy asserts that the instrument of choice for discovering Truth should be in the form of reasoned arguments and not of papal edicts or sacred texts. The fact that we are prone to question when confronted with something which we don't understand or agree with — such as the questions an ardent atheist might ask if ever given audience with the Pope — is testimony to our common need for reason's palliative effects. When confronted with differences of opinion or disputes, we commonly prefer to express our differing views though verbal or written communication, rather than to remain mute or resort to physical violence. I take this to be an indication of our innately rational nature. From this perspective therefore, arguing is a very good thing. Ideally arguments should resolve into a condition of mutual understanding if not agreement. And even though many might think of it as an uncomfortable, if not disreputable solution, "compromise" is often the ideal result of an earnest verbal jousting.

Thus if we consider the Pope's edict quoted at the beginning of this chapter as an apologetic thought experiment or an outright truth-claim, we might first ask: what role – if any – should reason play in establishing one's faith? If we claim that all religions are faith-based, this is not the same as saying that religions are totally absent of reason. All religious creeds offer some kind of rationale to support their beliefs and practices, no matter how absurd it may seem to those outside the faith. That being the case, what should be the essential guide towards a greater sense of human maturation and happiness – faith or pure reason? Or should we seek the kind of conciliation advocated by the Pope?

If we adopt the Pope's position, we might further ask if one aspect is more essential than the other in the pursuit of the good life. Saul of Damascus, who after his religious conversion was known as St. Paul, was an educated man steeped in the philosophy of Plato. Yet once he accepted Christ as his savior, he abandoned Greek philosophy altogether. It seems that his faith had overtaken any reliance he may have had on reason, at least in regard to his estimation of Truth itself. St. Augustine suggested that faith is a concern of our will (one's commitment to believe), whereas our rational beliefs testify as to how well our understanding comports with that faith. He also claimed that the only way to fully understand Christian doctrine was to first accept its creed as true beyond all doubt: in order to understand, he insisted, one must first believe, a distinct counterpoint to the philosophical view that one should reason first, thus establishing a foundation for examining the beliefs and truth-claims that follow.

Kierkegaard proposed what many would call a radical position in regard to the place of reason in the religious life: there is little to no place for it, for reason is divorced from the heartfelt courage that true faith requires of us. He was not an ignorant man. He was in fact a highly intelligent and educated individual. Yet he chastised the Christians of his time for having no actual faith, despite their church-

THE UNICORN PROBLEM

going ways and their adamant proclamations of Christian creed. According to Kierkegaard, Christians had hopelessly confused their obeisance to Church authorities with the true meaning of faith. They had become dogmatists, not authentic seekers of divine union with God.

He goes on to argue that any true Christian must first fully realize the profound desperation that attends every human life, how "fear and trembling" besiege the hearts of all human beings – how our souls are filled with a kind of existential sickness—an anomie and sense of dread that attends all of humanity. This pervasive sense of anxiety resides within us until the moment of death. Kierkegaard's position is that the healing of our soul's pain can come only through an unqualified full and true surrender to faith. I would suggest that this is but another way of addressing the Christian notion of original sin, as well as the Buddhist notion of the universal suffering of all sentient beings. Sartre would later characterize this sickness of the human psyche as the worm that lies coiled in the heart of nothingness.

Granted, none of this is a particularly uplifting portrayal of our innate dispositions, but keep in mind that from Kierkegaard's point of view humanity's fall from God's grace is quite real; it is an ontological fact. He realized that true faith cannot be found without acknowledging this lost connection to the divine. Humanity's fall from grace lies at the root of the desperation engendered in our hearts and minds. Faith must be born, as St. Augustine insisted, from the freely given assent of one's will. And though faith may be the ultimate form of irrationality, and the most unreasonable of acts, according to Kierkegaard, it is precisely this leap of faith into the abyss of absurdity that one must take.

In the view of Kierkegaard, the only recourse left to us in our search for Truth is subjectivity itself; the presence of subjectivity is a brute fact that offers up nothing less than a revelatory and foundational Truth. It is timeless, universal, necessary, and certain, and it can only be found within. Kierkegaard was in many ways echoing Tertullian's earlier claim that genuine faith was comprised of irrationality itself. Tertullian had argued that Christian doctrine has to be true. Why? Because of its absurdity: The various affronts to any reasonable considerations, such as a virgin birth or Jesus' resurrection from death, or consummately Jesus being the Son of God purposefully sent here to absolve humanity of its sins, was not to be considered a rational reproach of Christian doctrine, but instead served as its affirmation!

Many may find this argument itself absurd and that it can be easily dismissed. But I suspect that if a Zen Buddhist practitioner ponders the issue carefully, she might find herself in general agreement with Kierkegaard and Tertullian, (and ultimately with Jaspers) with reference to the claim that Truth will always elude any rational explanations. I have attended a number of Zen Sesshins, group Buddhist retreats where the goal is to discover one's true Buddha nature. The literal meaning of Sesshin is "heart-mind," and this intrinsic nature is believed to be the center of all sensation and cognition. Bringing one's internal state to a condition of stillness is the initial goal. As my Zen teacher once asked me: "What part of sit down and shut up don't you understand?" Come to think of it, he may have asked me that question more than once.

To clarify my above comments for those not familiar with Zen, I should explain that the basic practice of this Buddhist tradition involves sitting without movement or speaking for extended periods of time, using the stillness afforded practitioners as an opportunity to gain insight into the nature of the mind. I believe that Socrates would have wholeheartedly supported this practice, known as he was for standing motionless throughout the night outside his quarters during military campaigns, still as a Grecian statue while his comrades recovered from battle. His admonition regarding an examined life is reflected at Buddhist retreats at every moment of every day as aspirants seek answers to such questions as: Where do my thoughts come from, and where do they go? Where do my feelings come from, and where do they go? What lies beyond hope and fear?

Finding the answers to these big questions is the ultimate goal of this intensive meditative period, but the reality is that using one's

THE UNICORN PROBLEM

intellect as the transport for this endeavor is pointless. It is deemed a given that the rational mind is incapable of reaching the desired destination. All thoughts must be left behind if one is to step to the other shore. But if that's the case, then how do we get there? What will transport us to where we need to go?

The Buddhist answer comes in a variety of forms and methods, such as the cultivation of *calm-full abidance*, as described above, which ultimately leads the practitioner to the realization of the transient nature of all phenomena. Buddhists also refer to this process as resting in the empty nature of Mind, or depending on context, Establishing the View. Although there is no specific corollary to the monotheistic concept of faith in Buddhist doctrine, I contend that it is through this commitment to the attainment of one's Buddha nature that fidelity (faith) to the Buddhist orientation is established. At its core, faith and the realization of awakened mind are one and the same.

For most practitioners, gaining confidence in this newly acquired state of mind and ultimately securing the *groundless ground* of Buddhist metaphysics and ontology remains a demanding process. During meditation retreats practitioners very often break out in a rash of fitful weeping, uncontrollable laughter or other forms of anxious and neurotic behavior; each wrestles with his or her own experience of the fear and trembling accompanying the death of the ego. Once again, Jaspers, who was a student of Buddhism, would characterize this introspective process as the leap into transcendence. In addition, the Buddhist teacher D.T. Suzuki went so far as to say that the union with God that ardent Christians desire, and the simplicity of this transcendent state sought in a Buddhist Sesshin can be thought of as one and the same – Pure Awareness and God being two names for the same transcendent experience. (He also claimed that his spiritual name – The Great Simplicity – actually meant "The Great Stupidity," which to my mind places him in the great Socratic tradition of knowing precisely what he doesn't know.)

Depending on which sects we are considering, Buddhists or Hindus might also allude to supernatural realities, such as deities and

Pure Realms, all of this operating from the basic premise that Mind – not matter – is the ground of all existence. As mentioned previously, philosophy has sought explanations for life's mysteries predominately in the realm of nature, inferring that supernatural explanations are little more than an expression of our human ignorance, superstitions brought about by an insufficient understanding of the natural causes and conditions that produce our world. We should also keep in mind that this ignorance has the potential to engender violent acts, sanctioned travesties such as the Inquisition within the Christian Church. Although this line of separation between religion and philosophy is sometimes blurred (Medieval philosophy was oftentimes referred to as the "handmaiden of theology"), it remains fundamentally intact to this day.

Paradoxically, the ground of Reality for Plato and his philosophical descendants is what he termed Pure Forms. The Greek word for "form" translates to the English word "idea," so Plato was referring to the ontological reality of Pure Ideas. What are these Pure Ideas? They are the What is it? of things, of cats and dogs and mountains and the moon, but most especially of the intrinsic nature of The Good, Truth, Beauty, and Justice. Hence they are for most of us little more than pure Ideals.

Plato's belief was that everything that is in this earthly realm merely approximated these Ideals, imperfect imitations of the transcendent reality that serve as the pristine templates of their existence, the universal aspect of every particular object. Pure Forms are deemed more real than any knowledge or truths we may derive from our sense fields. Plato's premise was that these Forms exist independently, over and above the sense fields; or rather the sense fields are participants of the Pure Forms. In this way the archetypes of our existence remain transcendental, accessible to us only through the dialectic and perhaps a sudden rush of intuition brought about by the balancing of our sense driven impulses.

Bertrand Russell put it this way: "...This pure essence is what Plato calls an 'idea' or 'form' (It must not be supposed that 'ideas', in his sense, exist in minds, though they may be apprehended by minds).

THE UNICORN PROBLEM

The 'idea' justice is not identical with anything that is just: it is something other than particular things, which particular things partake of. Not being particular, it cannot itself exist in the world of sense. Moreover it is not fleeting or changeable like the things of sense: it is eternally itself, immutable and indestructible."

***

In parsing Plato's Pure Forms, we are alluding to an essentially immaterial aspect of being, to essences that incorporate such lofty Ideals as Beauty, Justice, and Truth. It's as though Plato is saying, "We do not have a Unicorn Problem; we have an idea of the Unicorn Problem." He did claim after all, that our thoughts were but the soul speaking to itself. But he has always had opponents.

Contrary to religious faith or even Plato's Pure Forms, the Milesian philosopher Thales (624-546) advocated a strictly naturalist view of knowledge, truth, and reality. Thales claimed that the world as we know it arises from a single, natural element: water. All life and all things spring from this primary source. Resorting to supernatural forces as a way of explaining existence is not necessary. He noted that when living beings perish they become dry and brittle, the primary element of water having escaped the desiccated forms. When the primary element of water dissipates, life has left with it. Adding to the store of knowledge attributed to Thales is his prediction of a solar eclipse in the year 585 BCE.

"This change from daylight to darkness had been foretold to the Ionians by Thales of Miletus, who fixed the date for it within the limits of the year in which it did, in fact, take place."

Twenty-five centuries later this feat has hardly been surpassed. We might naturally wonder: How he was able to do this? The source of his forecasting ability is still unknown (possibly Egypt), but it is extremely likely that he possessed the scientist's ability for keen observation and a geometric understanding of Nature and her supposedly inscrutable ways.

The natural philosophers that followed Thales disagreed with his designation of water as the primary element, or essence, of existence. Some claimed that the fundamental element is air, while others such as Heraclitus, argued for fire as the common source of all of Being. All of these claims and counterclaims became the basis of what we now refer to as 'soul theories' in both religion and philosophy. What animates a form to the extent that we say that it is sentient? Soul is one answer to this mystery, and that soul might very well be composed of nature's most primary element. Thales went so far as to say that the world is full of Gods, since, as he stated, god is nothing other than the soul, that which animates all living things.

"Thales, too, to judge from what is recorded of his views, seems to suppose that the soul is in a sense the cause of movement, since he says that a stone [magnet, or lodestone] has a soul because it causes movement to iron" ; "Some think that the soul pervades the whole universe, whence perhaps came Thales's view that everything is full of gods." (*De An.* 405a20-22)

So the overriding philosophical and theological question became: Is the soul, that animating force of life itself, natural or supernatural in origin? What is the avenue through which we might understand life's essential mysteries – faith or reason?

What is remarkable about these ancient philosophical views is how contrary they run to common sense, the information we naturally receive via our sense fields. In this way, their views were quite un-natural. What we experience normally is an infinite variety of nature's manifestations, from inanimate entities like rocks, to sentient beings like beetles (which comprise a quarter of all known species), to the human beings who study them. And this still doesn't account for the trillions of microorganisms that hide in plain sight. Why would anyone suspect a common source for all of this, when our senses demonstrate nothing but a vast, seemingly unending parade of unique entities – each with its own attributes (size, color, texture, taste, smell, etc.) – some sentient…but most not? Why would anyone suspect one common cause for a world that appears to be filled with nothing but an unending complexity of differentiated forms and functions?

THE UNICORN PROBLEM

And yet it seems that Thales' view of water, as the common element of all existence, wasn't that far off the mark: H2O can be found in just about everything, rocks included (albeit in minute amounts). And isn't water what we look for when exploring the other planets in our solar system, assuming that without this element life itself could not arise? Water it seems is a necessary condition, if not a sufficient condition, for the appearance of life.

Contemporary science also informs us that reality is quite different from what we perceive. Some philosophers, such as Locke, Hume, and Bishop Berkeley (1685-1753) questioned whether matter actually exists in the heart of existence at all, since we certainly don't perceive it. What we do perceive are the effects of some presumed, unseen substance that purportedly powers the entire sensorial display. Bishop Berkeley went so far as to argue that God, not matter, is the ground of all phenomena, much as Buddhists speak of Mind Only as the primary nature of reality. Berkeley's maxim was: "To be is to be perceived." (Latin: *esse est percipi*).

Perhaps, some philosophers speculated, this reference to a material "stuff" at the core of everything might simply be a logical inference; we feel compelled to make this leap (of faith?) given the sense-driven evidence before us. There must be some common substance that holds everything together and provides the power by which our sense fields are stimulated in the first place. When I look at the cup in my hand and list its attributes, its color, shape, weight and so on, I assume there must be something that 'glues' all these attributes into one form and conclude that this binding stuff is matter itself. Matter is the primary substance of not just the cup, but of all existing forms. Unfortunately, matter is never directly witnessed. Rather it is matter's effects that we encounter, leaving us at least one step removed from what is actual and real: the underlying substance itself.

Regardless of the truth of the matter, it is somewhat ironic that our current scientific view of natural phenomena is sounding more supernatural everyday, constantly leaping beyond the boundaries of our ordinary perspectives. It makes little common sense for instance, to be told that the leaves we see are not green and the sky is not blue, or that the earth circles the sun, and not the way these things actually appear to every normally functioning human being. That may be how it appears to us, we are told, but that's not how it really is. The mechanics of reality and the appearance of reality seem to be quite distinct from one another.

Science, both ancient and modern, has eclipsed our everyday view of reality by peering behind the chimera of appearances. The goal of science is to understand ordinary sense data not by how they appear to us, but rather by the principles that generate phenomena in the first place. It seems that the only vexing problem that remains for science is how to prove — in the strict sense of that word — that its theories are in fact completely sound. Science is still left with the epistemological issue of determining what constitutes certain knowledge — that about which it could not possibly be wrong.

Since science is continuously involved in the correction of its own errors, certain knowledge may well remain forever beyond its grasp, a self-imposed limitation predicated by its own method of inquiry. The philosopher Thomas Reid (1710-1796) would strongly disagree with this assessment.

He states: "We ought never to despair of human ability. Rather, we should hope that in due course it will produce a system of the powers and operations of the human mind that is just as certain as the systems of optics and astronomy."

It is worth noting that those individuals we refer to as scientists today were originally referred to as natural philosophers. The term *scientist* did not come into common usage until the mid 19th century. If the ancient natural philosopher Thales were alive today, we would refer to him as a scientist, and more specifically, an empiricist and mathematician — as one who believes that the source of all knowledge resides in the sense fields. We would not refer to him as a philosopher as we commonly use the term today. And a scientist by definition studies nature, not religious texts, in order to understand the world (which is not to suggest that all scientists are non-religious).

Religious leaders have only recently allowed scientific

discoveries to alter or influence Christian doctrine. The Catholic Church now accepts scientific discoveries as a viable source of knowledge and truth (with a small t), but only because the Church believes that when scientists dig into nature's core, they are simply revealing the majesty of God's works and all that He has created. On the Buddhist side of the equation, the Dalai Lama has recently stated that if science eventually shows the fundamental doctrines of Buddhism to be in error, Buddhism will have to change its doctrine. Which invites yet another question: Could science ever disprove the existence of God or the Buddhist doctrine of reincarnation? The straightforward answer is no – but we'll have more to say on this later.

To a die-hard scientist, if I claim that God exists, or even if I claim that God does not exist, both claims are considered vapid propositions. Scientists retain their own rules as to what constitutes reliable evidence for the validation of any hypothesis, theory, or belief; and that evidence must be in some manner observable, measurable, and accessible to empirical confirmation. God-talk offers no method to prove or disprove God's existence, no positive manner by which to determine the truth (or falsity) of conclusions regarding his existence or lack thereof. The same holds true for Buddhist proclamations about past and future lives, although the 20th century philosopher Friedrich Nietzsche (1844-1900) suffered a panic attack of sorts once he concluded that endless cycles of personal, human rebirth (what he termed the "eternal recurrence") might indeed be true. It was as though he had discovered a cosmic iteration of the movie Groundhog Day with its theme of déjà vu all over again.

To the natural philosopher, any claims regarding other worldly existence, be it in Heaven or otherwise, are considered speculation at best and, more often than not, pure nonsense. Even though God's existence is logically possible (it implies no logical contradiction if he does not), the postulation remains unverifiable. It is as they say, a "non-starter" – and an obvious candidate for Unicorn status. The contemporary physicist Stephen Hawking (1942-) puts a more refined point on the matter when he states that God's existence may be possible, but it is certainly not necessary.

This is not to say that theologians and other true believers have not tried to argue for the necessity of God. Indeed there are at least four different ways in which God's existence has been argued for in the Western theological traditions, as well as numerous arguments in the Eastern traditions for the existence of, alternately, a Divine Ground (Dharmakaya), a Brahman, the Great Tao, and so on.

In the West we have:

> 1) St. Thomas Aquinas's cosmological arguments (borrowed in main from Aristotle, with one significant revision);
>
> 2) Analogical arguments, such as proposed by William Paley, which has become a primary support for the current Intelligent Design argument;
>
> 3) The a priori, deductive proof of God's existence as proffered by St. Anselm; and finally,
>
> 4) The moral argument, i.e. without God there can be no moral truths.
>
> (We will examine some of these arguments in more detail later in this book.)

***

Consider the following excerpts from *Pensées,* (part III, §233):
> 1) "God is, or He is not.
>
> 2) A game is being played, where heads or tails will turn up.
>
> 3) In accordance with your reasoning, you can defend either of those propositions.
>
> 4) You must wager. (It's not optional.)

THE UNICORN PROBLEM

5) Let us weigh the gain and the loss in wagering that God *is*. Let us estimate these two chances. If you gain, you gain everything; if you lose, you lose nothing.

Wager, then, without hesitation that He is…

"…There is here an infinity of a happy life to gain, a chance of gain against a finite number of chances of loss, and what you stake is finite. And so our proposition is of infinite force, when there is the finite to stake in a game where there are equal risks of gain and of loss, and the infinite to gain."

Given this wager, formulated by the 17th century mathematician, philosopher, and Christian apologist Blaise Pascal (1623-1662), we are all left with two choices: one is to believe in God, and the other is not to believe. I would argue that what he is calling forth here is not so much belief but faith. I could believe, for example, that it is going to rain today. After all, I can see the dark clouds overhead, the wind kicking up, and the meteorologist, basing her forecast on her expertise, said to expect rain. There is ample evidence – not foolproof of course – that rain is on the way. I don't have faith it will rain but rather believe it will rain based on the evidence (reasons) before me. In the wager above we are being asked to believe that God exists, to accept God's existence, with no evidence offered to support this claim. This is the primary reason I feel Pascal is speaking of faith in God as opposed to believing in the existence of God: it is a conviction based on little to no evidence. So we could also complain that Pascal is committing the fallacy of begging the question right out of the gate. For our purposes in considering Pascal's wager, however, we will stick with the term *belief*. But the question remains: Why should anyone believe in something that supersedes or ignores any and all calls for justification?

Here's where Pascal steps in with what appears to be the most rational of arguments as to why we should believe that God exists.

But we should make clear that Pascal begins by establishing that reason cannot decide this issue for us.

In note 273, he says: "If we submit everything to reason, our religion will have no mysterious and supernatural element. If we offend the principles of reason, our religion will be absurd and ridiculous."

He goes on to say: "We are incapable of knowing either what [God] is or whether he is... Reason cannot decide this question. Infinite chaos separates us. At the far end of this infinite distance a coin is being spun which will come down heads or tails. How will you wager?"

If this is indeed the case, then we might ask: *Wager what?*

There are two wagers at stake here: the True and the Good. If we wager that God does in fact exist, which is to say that we believe in God's Being, what Good do we gain? Eternal happiness with our Heavenly Father. If in fact our belief is misplaced and God does not exist, what do we lose? Beyond some severe distress and crushing disappointment...not much.

Now let's consider the obverse: If we believe in God and he exists, again we gain everything and Truth has been affirmed. But if we don't believe in God, and in fact he does exist...uh-oh! Our troubles are just beginning. Therefore the rational person would choose to believe, despite the obvious fact that this belief might be false (Buddhists might deem their belief in karma as a similar kind of wager).

We should keep in mind that Pascal's Wager was never intended as a proof of God's existence. Rather it is a bet on immortality (the final reward in nearly all religious systems), since it is only God who guarantees eternal life. And the rational person, Pascal supposes, will take the best odds with the greatest stated pay-off. He is basing his belief in God on probability, not certainty. Most of us would have to admit that an eternal life of perpetual happiness is the greatest pay-off possible. Despite his protestations to the contrary, it seems that Pascal was attacking the ancient quest for certainty, especially regarding religious issues, through the use of reason. His views were instrumental in the later development of probability theory in mathematics. We also find that Pascal foreshadows the pragmatic perspectives of the philosophers Charles Pierce (1839-1914), William James (1842-1910), and of John Dewey (1859-1952) here in America.

We can, however, critique Pascal's wager from a couple of different angles. First, it seems that if we do assume the posture of belief in this regard and say that God does indeed exist, that is all we are doing: posturing. Wouldn't a divine being such as God with all his resplendent powers, especially his omniscience, know that we are feigning belief and truly have no faith? And worse yet, that these beliefs are being adopted for our own personal gain? It seems that believing in God's existence for the sake of a pay-off turns God's heaven into the Great Casino in the Sky, taking us far away from that species of faith a Christian such as Kierkegaard would admonish us to adopt. The very notion of accepting belief in God's existence for the sake of hitting the big jackpot in Heaven seems to contradict the very definition and intent of Christian doctrine.

Yet another criticism is this: Even though Pascal's wager offers us 50/50 odds, which aren't that unreasonable, those odds shift dramatically if we allow the possibility of more than one God. What about the God(s) of the Vedas, the Demiurge of Plato, the Pagan Gods of ancient Rome, or for that matter the gods of the South Sea Islanders or any other polytheistic religion we could name? The list of possible Creators would alter the odds so significantly that no reasonable person would take Pascal up on his wager. He's betting on one God only – his God. The rest of us might consider a wider range of possibilities and draw a different conclusion, reasonably deciding that all bets are off.

William James offers us another vantage point on the problem of belief or faith, different in many respects from Pascal's but equally intriguing. Before we examine James's position, some background information might be in order. In general we may adopt three basic positions in regard to God's existence (Note: Once again, we could substitute Buddha Mind for God). We may believe God exists, hence taking the position of theists; we may believe God doesn't exist – the position of atheists; or we may adopt the position of the English mathematician and philosopher, William Clifford (1845-1879) and conclude that reason compels us to be agnostic – and suspend judgment either way on the matter.

Clifford offers us a thought experiment to substantiate his position: Imagine, he says, a ship owner who is about to send a vessel full of immigrants to sea. He knows she's seen better days, needs repairs, and quite possibly may not be seaworthy at all. Doubts begin to fill his mind and he considers refitting her before the journey. He manages to overcome his doubts however, rationalizing that divine providence will protect these families on their trip from one continent to another. He ends up watching his ship's departure with a light heart, confident in his belief that all will be fine. And when the ship sinks in the high seas and all the immigrants drown, he retains his belief in the greater wisdom of providence and proceeds to collect his insurance money.

Clifford draws the following conclusion from this thought experiment: "The question of right and wrong has to do with the origin of his belief, not the matter of it; not what it was, but how he got it; not whether it turned out to be true or false, but whether he had a right to believe on such evidence as was before him."

In other words, the ship owner's belief on the seaworthiness of his vessel was not justified based on the evidence before him. Faith, which is belief without any evidence that would justify that belief, has no standing for Clifford in this instance.

And although James, in his book *The Will to Believe*, attacks Clifford's overall view, he does agree with the one of two rules that Clifford maintains should oversee all beliefs:

> 1) If a person is aware of evidence against a claim and there is no reliable evidence in support of it, to believe in that claim for personal reasons is wrong.
>
> 2) If there is no evidence for or against a belief, we have a duty to suspend judgment (remain agnostic).

THE UNICORN PROBLEM

It is with this second rule that James disagrees. Whenever we are confronted by a hypothesis that is intellectually indeterminable (i.e., whenever we confront a Unicorn), we have the right to follow our judgment and decide what to believe with one caveat: we must be confronted with a 'genuine option.' James' definition of a genuine option is three-fold: it must be living, momentous, and forced. A decision is *living* if it contains a real emotional appeal for us, if we can see either option as having real possibilities for us in our lives. James says that if we were to be offered the option of adopting a belief system that is personally untenable, it would be a *dead* option for most people. But if we were offered a choice that is of a personal option, for example in the West, between being agnostic or Christian, for most of us this would be a living decision.

To decide whether or not to believe in the reality of God or Buddha Mind is momentous, for serious consequences necessarily follow from that decision regardless of which side we may fall on. And finally, it is *forced* because the result of deciding and not deciding at all could very well be the same. As the philosopher William L. Rowe (1931-2015) points out, being offered an important job and being given a deadline to accept or reject the offer is a forced offer. The reason it is forced, in the sense that James maintains, is because to reject the offer or to not respond to the offer will lead to the same consequence: no job.

Overall, James' view is that no rule compels us to choose any of the policies Clifford has outlined. There is no duty to follow one prescription over another. We have the right to believe as we wish regarding these issues. I would agree with James, but I would also add that we have no right to force others to agree with our beliefs. Believe what you like, but allow me to draw my own conclusion as long as I intend no harm from it. The main point in James' argument returns to his initial premise: If the argument over God's existence or the reality of Buddha Mind is intellectually indeterminable, what recourse is left to us – belief in Unicorns?

***

MITCHELL J. FRANGADAKIS

Finally, we should consider the classic interpretation of the faith/reason debate as proffered by St. Augustine. We are already familiar with Plato's definition of knowledge, which is a belief that is both true and justified. We also agree with St. Augustine, in that belief alone is not sufficient to be termed as knowledge, even though it may be true. He argues that when we are compelled by reason to assent to a proposition, it qualifies as knowledge. This is so because the assent has been given as an act of reason alone rather than by verbal coercion or physical force. Knowledge is a 'truth claim' which reason compels us to accept, and it is in this sense that it is not truly a free act. If we are on a jury and the evidence compels us to accept that the defendant is guilty, our free will is not part of the decision-making process. Knowledge has the capacity to overturn our will. Beliefs or opinions alone, Augustine would argue, lack compelling evidence or a valid system of justification and do not qualify as knowledge. By definition beliefs and opinions are never certain; they are necessarily pluralistic. This view is quite similar to Plato's perspective.

Where Plato and St. Augustine part ways is on the issue of faith. Augustine argues that Christian faith does not require sufficient evidence to compel our assent through reason. Instead faith compels our assent by a *free act of our will*. We will ourselves to have faith. Why? Because there are sacred truths that exceed all the ability of human reason. Thus, according to Augustine, we believe in order to understand, not the other way around.

I know that my own mentor in Vajrayana Buddhism often asks the sangha if they have faith in the Buddhist teachings. Without faith, he admonishes, no real progress on the spiritual path is possible. If you don't have faith in the teachings and the words of the Buddha, he tells us, why bother showing up at all? Admittedly, neither I nor anyone else has had the temerity to press him on what exactly he means by faith, but I would assume it is not far removed from the faith of any spiritual adept within any religion. A significant difference remains however, since the notion of faith in Buddhism is

THE UNICORN PROBLEM

closely linked to an intimate understanding of the nature of impermanence and the empty nature of Being.

Public discourse on the issue of faith is inordinately difficult. Aside from our differing opinions as to what we might mean by the term, I find the problem to be one of privileged access only, i.e. it is a fundamentally subjective problem. It is an issue of value as much as fact, or rather the means by which we determine our values, which very often have little or nothing to do with rational thought. Most often the heart leads us in these matters. Or perhaps St. Augustine is more on track here when he tells us that faith is an act of will first, and the intellect follows because it must.

Traditionally, having religious beliefs means accepting them on the basis of faith, not reason. I think that the intrinsic meaning of faith, regardless of which religious tradition we address, requires an opening of the heart, a bursting of the psychic bonds that keep us from realizing our innate, primordial nature (as any good Buddhist might claim). Whether that inner nature is also the Truth of all that is, a syncretism of the Universal Good, or God, is not really the question here. Faith remains the vehicle, not the goal. In both Christianity and Buddhism, faith is required for that fearful journey within…returning to the union with the divine. And paradoxically, faith is also required if we are to follow Socrates' lead and reasonably examine our lives, in order to discover our moral compass and simultaneously gain a sense of meaning in our lives and in the world.

CHAPTER 6
LOGIC AND OTHER PRESUPPOSITIONS

"All human beings, by their very nature, desire to know."
Aristotle

"Mary is a brilliant scientist who is, for whatever reason, forced to investigate the world from a black and white room via a black and white television monitor. She specializes in the neurophysiology of vision and acquires, let us suppose, all the physical information there is to obtain about what goes on when we see ripe tomatoes, or the sky, and use terms like 'red', 'blue', and so on. She discovers, for example, just which wavelength combinations from the sky stimulate the retina, and exactly how this produces *via* the central nervous system the contraction of the vocal chords and expulsion of air from the lungs that results in the uttering of the sentence 'The sky is blue'. ...What will happen when Mary is released from her black and white room or is given a color television monitor? Will she *learn* anything or not? It seems just obvious that she will learn something about the world and our visual experience of it. But then is it inescapable that her previous knowledge was incomplete. But she had *all* the physical information. *Ergo* there is more to have than that, and Physicalism is false."
Frank Jackson 1982

THE UNICORN PROBLEM

FEEDING UNICORNS

Most of us feel assured that Unicorns don't exist. Despite the distant claims of a few, no one has ever seen a Unicorn, outside of perhaps a dream or in an artist's imaginative rendering. What we mean when we say that something 'exists' is that it has a reality independent of our perception of it. So even though most humans have never perceived the dark side of the moon, no one seriously thinks that it doesn't exist, in the fullest sense of that word. When we say we experience our existence, by definition, we are referring to a Reality (the way it is) independent of all minds, with the possible exceptions of God's Mind or Buddha-Mind.

"...The object is something that presumably exists independent of the subject's perception of it. In other words, the object would "be there," as it is, even if no subject perceived it. Hence, objectivity is typically associated with ideas such as reality, truth and reliability." – *I.E.P.*

Hypothetically however, the logical possibility of a Unicorn's existence is not out of the question. Logic allows that either side of the equation is possible: Even if we agree that Unicorns don't currently exist, it implies no inherent contradiction to propose that they could (at some time) exist. What does express a flat-out contradiction is that a square circle exists, that bachelors can be married men, or that Socrates or any other man is immortal. To be a man is to be mortal – by definition.

In a like fashion, we could adopt the same position in regard to God's existence. It is logically consistent to say that God could exist. We have no direct evidence of his existence (some would argue otherwise), but it is not irrational to say that we could in the future obtain this evidence. He could conceivably show up tomorrow in a chariot made of pure golden light, pass judgment on us all, and speedily determine our appropriate and eternal destinations. If this were to happen, we would all bear witness to his existence in the same way that we bear witness to the world we inhabit – via the sense fields. Granted, this fictional account of God's possible existence is very unlikely, but not impossible.

Now if we posit that it is logically possible for Unicorns to exist or that God or Buddha Mind could exist, the essential problem remains the same: what suffices as proof? What criteria are acceptable in determining their real or unreal status? Might any of these concepts ever be instantiated as an ontological fact? If so...how?

Another way of posing the same problem would be to ask: Is it possible for these potential entities to exist independently of our minds, or does reality necessarily require a witness? Science offers us the notion of objectivity, but what is meant by this term? Are we speaking of mathematical measurements that are used in science and technology all the time? Or do we mean to imply that our minds directly perceive nature's reality and our concepts inherently possess a one-to-one relationship with existential facts themselves? Most scientists, until the post-modern deconstructionist period, would argue that science is revealing reality directly – what science is claiming as a truth of nature is simply that, a factual description of a world that exists and operates independently of us; all of humanity could disappear, but the world would continue on without us.

St. Augustine would disagree with this assessment of scientific prowess. He argues: "...For every science proceeds from self-evident principles. But sacred doctrine proceeds from articles of faith which are not self-evident, since their truth is not admitted by all..."

Augustine is concerned with separating the Truth of the sacred doctrine from natural philosophers' criteria for truth and reality. Science may offer contingent truths agreed by all, but this is not the final Truth revealed to us through Holy Scripture. In his view, a sacred doctrine cannot be judged through the normal, scientific methods of inquiry. Most religions, including Buddhism, would concur with this position. (It may not be explained, however, in the same manner). After all, the good Saint appears to be begging the question, but most religious believers would draw similar conclusions, accepting revealed scripture to be the final word on Truth and Reality.

Serious consequences may follow however, if we choose to ignore reason or logic altogether. Aristotle's second Law of logic stipulates that whatever exists cannot both be and not be simultaneously. If I claim that the cup from which I am currently sipping coffee does not exist, I am obviously violating this Law. Following this type of violation in basic logic, the Principle of Explosion states that: "from a contradiction, anything follows" (Latin: *ex falso quodilbet*).

Examples of this principle abound in today's media, from advertisements to talking heads on the flat screen. One example I recall involved the newscaster Glenn Beck on Fox News. In a roundtable discussion with his fellow "journalists", Beck stated that our current and first black President, Barack Obama, is a racist. Less than two minutes later, he contradicts his own previous statement. "I am not saying," he reported, "that Barack Obama is a racist." We are left to wonder which of his two statements we are to believe. It seems obvious that anything could follow from those reported statements: yea or nay…or in this instance both. No clear conclusions here, either for logic or common sense.

Any serious proposal should be thought of as a flagpole thrust into the ground, a place where a person takes a stand and necessarily runs the risk of standing corrected or being run over. If I say, "the cup is" and then contradict myself by insisting that, at the same time, "the cup is not"; if I take a position and immediately negate that position, then how is any reasonable dialogue even possible? In the example above, does Beck believe that President Obama is a racist or not? Which of his two contradictory claims should we hold him to? That said, I might add that it is very difficult in day-to-day life not to contradict oneself. But we shouldn't sculpt irrationality into a craft for selling sloppy thinking on the airwaves or anywhere else, for that matter.

Apropos of the point I'm making – and though there aren't that many good jokes about Philosophy – here's one that illustrates the issue: In a final exam, a philosophy professor asked for a 500-word essay explaining how it is that the chair he was sitting in *does not exist*. No doubt he was expecting some of Locke's analysis of 'primary and secondary qualities,' or perhaps one of Bishop Berkeley's arguments as to how an object does not exist unless it is perceived; that to be is to be perceived. A young lady sitting in the front row of the class instantly scribbled some words in her blue book, turned it in and left with a big smile on her face. Curious as to how she could have finished so quickly, and completely prepared to flunk her, the professor opened her exam. Inside, the young student of philosophy had written: *What chair?*

For those more interested in reasoning for the sake of non-deceptive communication, the Principle of Explosion can be placed into symbolic terms in the following way:

Where: "¬" symbolizes the relation of logical consequences

$$\{\emptyset, \neg \emptyset\} \pm \vdash \uplus$$
$$\text{or}$$
$$\bot \to P$$

This can be read as: "If one claims something is both true (∅) and not true (¬ ∅), one can logically derive *any* conclusion (⊎)."

In summary, two contradictory premises enable us to infer the conclusion we prefer (or believe) to be true.

The appropriate understanding and application of logic offers us a way around these types of contradictory claims. For example, what are referred to as *a priori* arguments lead us to conclusions that are necessarily true. The term *a priori* means prior to sense impressions or perceptions—therefore, an argument based on deductive logic alone. For a simple example, if someone informs me that there are a number of bachelors in the room next to mine, I do not have to enter that room in order to know (beyond all doubt) that those men in the room are unmarried. It is true by definition, hence a priori. If however, someone were to ask me how many bachelors are in the room next door, I would have to go and look. This is knowledge after the fact, *a posteriori*. A posteriori arguments, such as the Cosmological Argument or Teleological Argument that attempt to prove God's existence, are dependent on empirical evidence to support their ultimate claim.

We should also clarify the term *proof* and recognize that it has a technical meaning in the game book of logic. A proof of a proposal, such as "God (or Buddha Mind) exists" can only result from a deductive argument, and this argument must be both valid and sound. *Valid* in this context means that the reasons offered as evidence actually do substantiate the claim; the conclusion follows logically from the premises given. There are no obvious non-sequiturs in the argument, i.e. no illogical inferences are being made.

A sound argument must be valid in the above sense, and the reasons that substantiate the claim (the premises) must themselves be true. Ultimately, the premises proffered must be accurate and trustworthy. In some instances however, the premises or reasons proffered may be considered self-evidently true. If I claim that Socrates is mortal, this claim follows necessarily from the accepted truth that all men are mortal – notwithstanding claims about Jesus of Nazareth and quite a few lesser-known individuals.

Self-evident truths, such as Euclid's Axioms in geometry, eliminate the logical problem of an infinite regress, the endless search for evidence that requires no further justification. True evidence is accepted as factual, much in the same way that 1=1 is accepted as factual (Law of Identity). Hence when Euclid provided us with his geometric demonstrations, his conclusions were necessarily true, since the premises (the axioms) were already assumed to be true, and he didn't violate any obvious rules of deductive logic in reaching his conclusions.

What is not so obvious is our uncritical acceptance of his fundamental definitions, axioms, and postulates, those primary principles (or as Descartes might assert, the "clear and distinct ideas") that stand beyond our criticisms or refutations. Another way of saying this is that they are basic beliefs, foundational propositions that we accept as true without further question. For example, at the present moment I am supremely confident that *I am in my living room right now*. What justification for this claim is necessary? Most would answer: "none." It is not only a basic, self-evident belief, but also – as the contemporary philosopher Alvin Plantinga (1932-) might say – a *properly basic belief* (PBB). Complementing this view, Russell might argue that my relationship (or as he terms it, my "acquaintance") with the room is immediate and therefore not subject to error. It is neither true nor false that I am in the room, since the fact of existing at all is deemed "self-evident."

While the certainty of our conclusions in logical, deductive arguments – the subsequent transfer of our premises into truth-bearing claims – depends on the validity of our logic, the necessary truth of our conclusions depends on the veracity of our premises. So we might wonder: why are those premises—such as Euclid's axioms—to be thought of as true? What other reasons do we have to claim that they are indeed beyond refutation? And if we decide not to accept Euclid's self-evident truths, or go so far as to reach into political and moral domains and question whether or not our Constitutional guarantees of "...life, liberty, and the pursuit of happiness..." or that "all men are created equal" are as obvious as claimed, then we seem to be pulled into a circle of endlessly justifying our justifications. This is what is meant by "infinite regress", and the Oxford dictionary defines it this way: "A sequence of reasoning or justification which can never come to an end."

Aristotle spoke of this problem, stating: "Some hold that, owing to the necessity of knowing the primary premises, there is no scientific knowledge. Others think there is, but that all truths are demonstrable. Neither doctrine is either true or a necessary deduction from the premises…"

In his *Posterior Analytics* (Book 1, part 3) he draws his own conclusion: "…Our own doctrine is that not all knowledge is demonstrative: on the contrary, knowledge of the immediate premises is independent of demonstration. (The necessity of this is obvious; for since we must know the prior premises from which the demonstration is drawn, and since the regress must end in immediate truths, those truths must be indemonstrable.)"

I have elaborated on this tautological feature of general epistemology because the infinite regress problem – along with various forms of paradox – is one of the alpha specimens roaming throughout the *Unicorn Problem*. That said, it should be noted that there are at least three traditional responses to this epistemological conundrum:

1) *Foundationalism*:

Some beliefs are justified because they serve as the foundation upon which other beliefs are justified. For example, Descartes' "cogito ergo sum" is a foundational belief which is accepted as true, requiring nothing to support it. It is a *basic belief*. As already noted, Plantinga secures his theological claims on properly basic beliefs.

2) *Coherentism*:

Beliefs are justified by other beliefs, but the circular nature of these arguments is allowed. There is a regress of sorts, but it is not infinite. Instead, the critical issue becomes whether one's beliefs are consistent with one another, whether one's system of various beliefs mutually support one another. For example, I believe that other people have a mind in the same way that I have a mind. This belief is supported by the belief in the truth of my own mental experiences. And accepting all of this as true does not conflict with my other belief systems. I might not be right, but at least I'm consistent.

3) *Skepticism*: There are no justified beliefs; hence, Plato's claim that *knowledge is a justified, true belief* is claiming the impossible.

We should bear in mind that the infinite regress problem is not restricted to only logical or philosophical issues. All systems of knowledge, including both scientific and religious doctrines, are obliged to offer some minimal standard of verification for their truth-bearing claims. Without that, the truth-claims would no longer be claims about truth, but rather articles of belief or faith. The actual type of proof required might vary depending on the event or issue we are considering; i.e., it may not be the deductive certitude we find in logical demonstrations. But it could be the reliable, inductive conclusion: "Since the sun always appears on the eastern horizon in the morning, tomorrow's sunrise will also occur on the eastern horizon."

All truth-bearing claims, regardless of their source, are derived from premises that are assumed to be true – taken for granted as the way things "really are" – and are therefore often deemed foundational, or to once again borrow Plantinga's term: a properly basic belief. A foundational premise functions as a purchase on which other beliefs can be mounted. All knowledge systems rely upon some kind of basic assumptions, sometimes consciously (as with the quotes from St. Augustine and Aristotle above), but most often unconsciously. If this is indeed the case, it would seem that any form of truth is a judgment founded on practical considerations more so than any given, self-evident reality.

A critical analysis of primary assumptions held by any knowledge system is one of philosophy's primary tasks. *Why* those assumptions are taken as self-evidently true is the fundamental question. And this is not just an epistemological problem. We find similar conundrums when searching for our essential nature, our true self-identity: If I claim: "This (fill in the blank)… is who I am," then we might ask: who is making this claim? Who is it that has drawn this conclusion? The answer is: "It is I, of course." But if it is always "I" claiming to know who I am, isn't this yet another instance of circular reasoning, and why can't the "foundational self" show itself once and for all? What position remains as the primary justification for my claim that I know who I am? How am I to justify this assumption that I actually possess a self-inherent being?

THE UNICORN PROBLEM

It seems our minds can reflect upon some notion of a true self or primary identity, but it does so through a prism reflecting infinite facets. Any claim that I know who I am rests on the assumption that I am the one who knows this...ad infinitum. We could of course attempt to circumvent the infinite regress problem by simply allowing an infinite set of reasons...beliefs supporting beliefs...from now until forever.

***

Rehearsing the fundamental rules of logic and argumentation, the consensus is that if the premises that support a claim are true and the logic coherent – i.e., has no fallacies or does not violate basic principles of logic – then the claim or conclusion is both necessary and certain. And, in this context, *certain* means that it is not possible to be wrong about this conclusion. If all of the above criteria are met, then an argument is termed *sound,* one in which one might place complete confidence.

The classic example (with slight variation) of a *certainly true claim* is:
  All men are mortal
  Socrates is a man.
  Therefore, it follows necessarily that Socrates has thrown off his mortal coil.

Hence if I accept, for example, the fundamental definitions of mathematics, it is impossible for me to be wrong when I claim that 4 plus 4 equals 8. However, if we were to switch to something other than 'base ten', thereby changing the rules of the math game, my totals would change accordingly. The determination to know the truth of any proposition, not with percentages of probability, but rather with complete certainty, was the goal of both philosophers and theologians from the time of Thales up through the modern period of human history. Truth must be logically deduced if it is to be known with certainty. The ultimate goal for all truth-seekers was –

and remains to some extent – knowledge that is timeless, universal, necessary and certain. It is *necessary* because the way one has played the logic game has violated no rules; no principles of logic have suffered any misapplications. And *certainty*, in this context, is absolute. This kind of logic will not accept the notion of almost certain, as scientists today oftentimes do. For example, the recent discovery of the 'Higgs boson' particle has been called "almost certain" by the scientific community. Deductive proofs don't allow this kind of variance. So the bar for logical certainty is set as high as possible and serves as the gold standard in epistemology. Skeptics would say no one has ever demonstrated this quality of knowledge, nor is it possible.

Even in a court of law, where an individual's welfare hangs in the balance, it is not expected that this standard for truth will be attained. Lawyers inform prospective jurors in a criminal trial case that the conclusion reached, guilty or not, must be "beyond a reasonable doubt." What does this mean? It means that it is the conclusions that a group of reasonable persons – in this instance, the jury – would come to, given the evidence presented. Court cases are by their very nature outside the formal definition of "proof" as given by logicians. In that sense, we never actually prove a defendant guilty or innocent. A jury's verdict is not a sound deductive demonstration. If the defendant's fingerprints are all over the murder weapon, the only definite conclusions possible are that the defendant handled the weapon or that someone transferred his prints to the weapon. Whether or not he or she actually did the deed is still open to argument. No matter how convincing the accumulation of evidence, unless we can begin with some universal premise that we can accept as 100% true (such as the fact that all men are mortal, or that bachelors are by definition unhitched), we cannot come to a necessarily true verdict, i.e. a proof.

Despite these concerns, most of us would agree that if we were accused and taken to trial for a crime we did not commit, we would prefer a jury of our peers making the decision as to our innocence or guilt, as opposed to the angry mob waiting for us

THE UNICORN PROBLEM

outside with a large dead-man's noose in their hands. Legal and moral issues always contain a certain amount of uncertainty, no matter how overwhelming the evidence might be (one or two shooters on the grassy knoll?).

What's at stake here is both truth and our understanding of reality, of what is actually occurring, as opposed to what our opinions or beliefs about the matter may be. No matter how well intentioned our motivations may be, reasonable arguments concerning moral or public policy, including criminal court cases, are never proven beyond all doubt. To insist, for example, that our country needs to invest in green energy is a policy claim that can't be proven as a necessary truth, but most reasonable people would probably agree that it is something our country should and must do. It appears to be beyond a reasonable doubt. Most of us would rely on experts to advise us in this matter, people who actually spend their lives studying the problem and who possess the ability to analyze the information. It seems that many people today take truth to be little more than a matter of opinion, and what makes my opinion truer than yours are not independent facts or evidence, but simply the fact that it's my opinion. Aristotle would be aghast at this way of thinking, since it has no place in the ethos of philosophy or reason.

If every truth and fact about reality is open to individual opinion and belief, then there must exist as many versions of truth and reality as there are individuals, or perhaps nothing that exists is real at all. As Socrates remarked, if all truth is relative, then why not ask any person we meet about wisdom? Isn't his or her opinion equal to even the most learned individual? If I were to rely on this attitude, then I might believe it reasonable for me to consult my auto mechanic to cure my toothache, and if my car won't start, then I suppose I could call my doctor. These are exaggerated examples of unsound reasoning, but they illustrate the point that not all opinions hold the same weight and not all truth is personal.

For most theologians and those philosophers whose allegiance dates back to the hyper-rationalism of Descartes and Plato, this proposition that all truth and reality is relative is not acceptable.

MITCHELL J. FRANGADAKIS

Truth is an independent creature, not susceptible to the wayward and shifting course of opinions and beliefs. Truth will be what it is regardless of whether human beings are around to acknowledge it or not. From the view of Plato's *Gods*, the Pythagorean Theorem will be true no matter if I agree with it or not, and furthermore, it will always be true, today, tomorrow…whenever.

In his *Proslogian*, St. Anselm (1033-1109 AD) of Canterbury offered his Ontological Argument, which he believed demonstrated, once and for all, the existence of God. In order to fully appreciate the force of St. Anselm's argument, we should first keep in mind that it is an a priori argument, which we now know means that the truth-claim is substantiated by logic alone. Because of this, it does not enforce its conclusion through any empirical evidence, unlike the Cosmological Argument of St. Aquinas, which posits a First Cause and so is an argument based on time, an empirical event which measures movement and changing relationships between objects in space. St. Anselm was seeking a proof for God's existence that fulfilled the formal definition of a proof in logic. He was seeking a Euclidian demonstration of a necessary and certain truth.

He was also dissatisfied with previous arguments that tried to substantiate God's existence, because they depended on empirical or a posteriori evidence. For example, the claims in the Cosmological Argument in Theology take us back to Aristotle's Prime or Unmoved Mover: Existence must have had a First Cause. This argument is sense-dependent, not the outcome of pure Reason. The story goes that St. Anselm spent weeks of sleepless nights during his quest for the perfect argument demonstrating the necessity of God's existence, to be proven by pure logic alone, and therefore was independent of conclusions based on sense perception. His fellow monks feared he had become possessed by some malevolent force, since he had stopped eating, grew thin and weak, and only recovered when the solution came to him in a dream.

I should add that the jury is still out on Anselm's purely logical proof of the necessity for God's existence. Some say that we cannot argue from concepts to reality, even if the logic is faultless. Others

THE UNICORN PROBLEM

insist that the argument is sound, but requires belief that God *might* exist…which is a bridge too far. Whether or not it is possible to move from concepts to reality is still a major divide in scientific and philosophical epistemology; i.e., arguments over what exactly constitutes knowledge.

What follows is the simpler version of St. Anselm's Argument.

1) Persons have the idea of a greatest possible being.

2) Suppose the object of this idea exists only as an idea in the mind.

3) Existence in reality is greater than existence only in the mind.

4) Therefore, we can conceive of a being greater than the greatest possible being, that is, a being who also exists in reality.

5) But there can be no being greater than the greatest possible being.

6) Therefore, the greatest possible being exists in reality.

The argument turns on premise #4, which leaves us with an absurdity, i.e., a logical contradiction; therefore we have #5, and the conclusion #6 that God exists in reality, not just as a concept.

Below is a more comprehensive version as given by Professor Rowe. A brief note first: I will follow Professor Rowe's advice and substitute the word "God" for St. Anselm's phrase: "…that than which nothing greater can be conceived." Moreover, I take that phrase to mean the concept of Perfection, since God is said to be by definition, perfect. This is the position of the modern Anselmians.

What we have is a major premise that seeks to define God (We could just as well employ the concept of Buddha Mind). If we agree to the definition, then it is supposed that if the claim follows coherently (logically) from the premises, and all the premises proffered are true, then the conclusion is necessarily true—it is deductively proved.

Here is a recast version of St. Anselm's Argument:

1) God exists in the understanding.

2) God might have existed in reality.

3) If something exists only in the understanding, and might have existed in reality, then it might have been greater than it is.

4) Suppose God exists only in the understanding.

5) God might have been greater than he is.

6) God is a being than which a greater is possible.

7) The being than which none greater is possible is a being than which a greater is possible.

8) It is false that God exists only in the understanding.

9) God exists in reality as well as in the understanding.

The underlying assumption in this argument, aside from the belief that God might exist, is the unexpressed belief in The Great Chain of Being. St. Anselm believed that there exists a *chain of being* or interconnectedness from the lowest levels of existence to the highest, with human beings somewhere in the middle – between beasts and angels. This was accepted knowledge in medieval times.

Vajrayana Buddhism offer a similar doctrine, the lower realms inhabited by "hungry ghosts," and higher realms filled with "Titans" (the Jealous Gods Realm) as well as Deities emanating from Pure Realms. Human beings, it is believed, have a fighting chance at liberation, sequestered somewhere in the midst of all this. Moreover,

THE UNICORN PROBLEM

for Buddhists all these diverse realms of being exist simultaneously, separated only by our karmic dispositions (Might this be a logical contradiction?). Buddhist teachings insist that the Dharmakaya subsists throughout every realm of existence—it is the ground of all realms of Being, no matter how alien they may sound to us. Moreover, knowledge of the Dharmakaya (Truth Body) is accessible to yogis through what is referred to as Direct Cognition, a type of religious or mystical experience we will explore in a later chapter.

A Christian Monk by the name of Gaunilo (1033-1109) took issue with the first premise in the St. Anselm's argument, saying it was necessarily false: i.e., that we cannot conceive of perfection, of that than which nothing greater can be conceived. We can always conceive of something greater…ad infinitum. Another criticism pokes at the word "greater." How do we know that something that exists is greater than that which is only conceived? Still others would argue that St. Anselm is simply equivocating, using the same word *greater* for two different ideas. Again it should be pointed out that St. Anselm is resorting to the Great Chain of Being to define his meaning of greater. His is a hierarchical view of existence, with God at the tippy-top—the godhead – and very bad places at the bottom. Immanuel Kant critiqued St. Anselm's argument by pointing out that existence is a given. If I say, "the cup is in my hand," I offer no new information if I then say "the cup in my hand exists"; it adds nothing to the first statement. Saying that something exists does not make it greater: its existence has been accepted as given.

***

When Parmenides, some two-thousand years ago, demonstrates through pure reason that no particle such as the "uncuttable" atom of Democritus and Leucippus can logically exist, which side should rational people like ourselves stand on? Go with logic or let the sense data do all the talking? Or does the blast produced by an atomic bomb answer that question for us? We are all left with this dilemma of deciding between various ways of determining the correct course we should follow at this crossroads in human history, and whether or not the human mind is capable of independently determining exactly what constitutes truth and reality. In other words: how will we know Reality if and when we find it?

As philosopher Alvin Goldman (1938-) points out in his lecture series, *Science Wars*, the discovery of radioactivity and the x-ray altered our picture of reality considerably, giving us actual x-ray vision. That was a distinctive change in our perception of the underlying picture of existence; we could now, like Superman in the comic books, see through things. Shoe stores were quick to put in x-ray machines for correct sizing, and we could look right through the leather of our shoes as well as the thin veil of our skin to peer directly at our foot bones (quite a sight for a five-year old!). Our discovery of fusion as the source of the sun's heat and light as opposed to simple chemical interaction was another momentous change in our understanding of reality. And not only do we circle that sun along with other planets, Hubble's discovery of Andromeda meant that there really is another galaxy out there besides ours, and who knows exactly how many billions more? The Italian philosopher, mathematician, and Dominican Friar Giordano Bruno (1548-1600) speculated that the sun was one star of an infinite number of stars, and that therefore there could be an infinite number of worlds populated by other intelligent beings. Perhaps, he concluded, we humans were not that special after all. His reward for such bold speculations was to be convicted of heresy and expediently burned at the stake in 1600.

The universe (Cosmos) in Aristotle's time was a closed, finite system. Since then, Einstein's Relativity theory has redefined the fundamental categories of space, time and motion, as well as the reality of matter, which he showed to be convertible with energy. Today we hypothesize about an infinite universe and even multiple universes – all of which are infinite. It seems that reality is perpetually being redefined by science. And as already noted, in the scientific world if an object is not defined, it does not exist.

So we return to the problem of determining what makes a

THE UNICORN PROBLEM

claim more than mere opinion? What is the difference between what I believe and what is actually the case? Plato himself proposed one answer to the question. What, he wondered, separates knowledge from mere opinion or belief?

A simple little thought experiment might help illustrate the criteria offered, clarifying what Plato meant when he said knowledge is a justified true belief (JTB):

Imagine a small boy passes by a candy shop. His spots a large, clear, glass jar filled with jellybeans sitting between rows and rows of chocolate candies. Next to the jar is a sign that says: "Guess how many jellybeans are in the jar! The right number will win a trip for you and your family to Hawaii!" The boy has always dreamed of going to Hawaii, so he persuades his mother to go with him to the candy store, and, with her help, fills out the entry form. He studies the jar very carefully and writes down the number 5,322. A week later the family receives notification that they have won the trip to Hawaii. The boy's studied belief that there were that many jellybeans in the jar turned out to be true.

So the question now is: Did the boy *know* how many beans were in the jar? And according to Plato's definition of knowledge, the answer would be: not really. And we would all agree, since though the boy might have truly believed his answer was correct, it was simply a lucky guess. He had no sufficient information or system of justification to back up his belief. So though his belief was proven true, it was obviously not justified. Now imagine that another similar contest were to be held. Do you think that the boy would win the contest yet again? He was simply a very lucky boy the first time.

We might now imagine how a scientist trained in optics, glassware, and the particular attributes of jellybeans would likely tackle the problem. He sees the same jar, breaks out his slide-rule (he's a traditionalist), and through a very sophisticated system of mathematics and scientific principles, calculates the amount of space in the jar and how much space each jelly bean occupies and/or displaces, thereby determining the correct number of beans in the jar.

He has an extremely sophisticated method of justifying his claim, and if another contest were to occur, he could simply apply this same method to ascertain with near certainty the number of beans in the second contest as well. The scientist as Plato has also asserted, doesn't simply believe his answer to be true; this trained researcher has the particular knowledge to decode the requirements posed in the problem and apply them to his solution. He operates a step above beliefs, opinions, and a great leap beyond blind luck.

How should we explain the obvious fact that logic leads us to more reliable judgments than mere guesses? Couldn't I assemble any concepts I desire if guesses or my opinions occasionally stumble into the truth? And if logic is little more than agreeable inferences from one proposition to another — much as Locke and Hume argued — then how do these ideas actually offer us peeps into Knowledge and Reality? Even though the little boy in the drugstore correctly determined the number of jelly beans in the jar, it is hard to argue that the scientific approach, based on research data, mathematics, logic and critical analysis, does not lead us to more valid and certain knowledge about the world.

I'm confident most would agree that this is a more reliable way to satisfy the human thirst for certainty and clarity regarding what we know and what we believe. However not everyone accepts Plato's criteria for knowledge. There is a philosophical camp that argues that there is also another form of knowledge determined by belief alone and this form of belief is unique in that it may also serve as a means of achieving *certain* knowledge. If you believe you are reading this text right now, despite the fact that you could be dreaming or exist as no more than a simulation in the Matrix — and you realize that you can't prove with absolute certainty that you're not — this is an example of a PBB employed as a foundation for epistemology. (We will address PBB's more fully in a later chapter.)

The Jewish rabbi and theologian Saadya Gaon (known in Arabic as Sa'id 'ibn Yasuf al-Fayyum (882-942 C.E.) suggests yet another source of reliable, certain knowledge, and that is knowledge based on trusted testimony.

THE UNICORN PROBLEM

"Saadya wants to be able to provide his readers with the capacity to *know truly and with certainty* because he wants to provide them a genuine space in which to *live truly and with certainty*."

For Saadya (contrary to what his position seems to indicate), the primary instrument for living this true and certain way of life was through reason. Yet faith appears to be a large part of that process as well. Saadya advances – as all religious systems do – revealed scripture as a reliable source of knowledge that, rather than contradicting reasonable conclusions, depends on our rational faculties in order to be fully appreciated.

He explains:"[God] knew that His laws and the stories of His wondrous signs would, through the passage of time, require people to hand them down to posterity, so that they might become as evident to later generations as they were to the earlier ones. Therefore, He prepared in our minds a place for the acceptance of reliable tradition (*al-kabar as-sâdiq*) and in our souls a quiet corner for trusting it so that His Scriptures and stories should remain safely with us."

This line of reasoning implies that reports passed down through the generations are narratives we can trust. We should accept these revealed truths as timeless, universal, and certain, for there is no reason for the original authors to lie. Their testimony is assumed to be reliable in the same sense that a child relies on the truthfulness of his or her parents. We should trust revealed scripture because it is natural to trust the accounts of people we know and rely upon. Scripture, according to Saadya, is an immediate source for certain knowledge. This is the assumption underlying all revealed theologies.

Once again, we return to the fundamental question in epistemology: What is knowledge, and how is it to be defined? If we say it requires no definition, no outlines or boundaries by which to fix it in our minds, then by the principle of explosion, knowledge could be anything we deem it to be. Indeed, alternative sources for trustworthy knowledge have been proposed, from trusting in pure faith to seeking a purity and clarity of life through the principles of logic alone. Many claim however, that human beings will always exist within a grand mystery, never possessing any truth beyond the practical judgments and conclusions of our mundane existence.

CHAPTER 7
FROM ILLUSION TO TRUTH

"I said to the almond tree: Speak to me of God, and the almond tree blossomed."
Nikos Kazantzakis (1883-1957)

"Henry drives through a rural area in which what appear to be barns are, with the exception of just one, mere barn facades. From the road on which Henry is driving, these facades look exactly like real barns. He happens, however, to be looking at the one and only real barn in the area and believes that there's a barn over there. When asked if he sees a barn, Henry replies that he does. The question remains: Does he really know it's a barn?"

HOW TO SADDLE A UNICORN

Since the most literal translation of the word *philosophy* is the love of wisdom, it would seem that religion and philosophy would have much in common. Both are systems founded on the search for the underlying truth regarding their respective systems of belief, and both share a deep conviction in the central role that truth and wisdom play in their respective disciplines. As Albert Einstein once remarked, "Science without religion is lame, and religion without science is blind".

They share other attributes as well. For example, both are contemplative in nature, and as a consequence both require a degree of leisure time, a relaxed step away from ordinary concerns. Examining a life requires that one allow sufficient time for self-reflection, prayer or meditation, as well as a rigorous critique of one's own thoughts and convictions. This is not the usual mode in the action-oriented, competitive spirit that both pervades and is promoted by our culture. In this sense, both religious practices and philosophical pursuits are impractical to the extreme. However since antiquity, both disciplines have continued in their quest for the ultimate Truth or Wisdom about which it would be impossible to be wrong. This quest led to various claims about God, Allah, Buddha Mind, Big Bangs and Boson Fields, each asserting in its own way the truth of the Immutable and thereby what constitutes our overarching metaphysical circumstances.

As the scholar of medieval philosophy Etienne Gilson (1884-1978) points out: "... when Augustine undertakes to describe existence in philosophical terms, he at once falls back on the Greek identification of being with the notions of immateriality, intelligibility, immutability, and unity. Every such thing is divine; since truth is such, truth is divine. Immaterial, intelligible, and immutable, truth belongs in the order of that which truly is, or exists. Consequently, it belongs to God."

Religion and traditional schools of both psychology and philosophy are also similar in their claims that human ignorance casts a long shadow over Truth and Reality. Socrates reminded us that anyone who willingly commits an injustice is not evil, but simply ignorant of his or her inherent nature, and thus has not yet realized that personal intimacy with the Pure Form of the Good. A sinner or evil person in the Christian sense would then be someone who has achieved this realization and despite this, transgresses against or violates that wisdom itself.

The persistent questioning of our basic assumptions has proven to be a useful philosophical tool in the quest for wisdom and abiding truth. A vivid example of how our definitions (or lack thereof) may lead us astray comes from the parable of "Buridan's Ass," a philosophical paradox constructed by the 14th-century philosopher Jean Buridan (1300-1358), regarding the consequences of indecision.

MITCHELL J. FRANGADAKIS

I have updated this story, but the general lesson to be learned remains the same: "Imagine Joe Smith has just left home for college. Joe is a 'fast-food' junkie, who finds himself living equidistant from his two favorite dining locales, Burger King and McDonalds. Since he has no reason to prefer one over the other, he finds that he can't make a decision as to where to eat. Each restaurant is the same distance away, and each provides the tasty giant-burgers that he so enjoys. So, with his stomach rumbling, he decides he'll simply flip a coin. But the problem with this solution is the solemn vow he had made to himself since entering college. As a consequence of some unfortunate past experiences, he had vowed that he would never make decisions based on irrational choices. He believes that flipping a coin is an irrational act, based on chance, not reason, and, therefore, not a permissible choice. What to do now? He needs to eat, but doesn't know how to resolve his dilemma."

As it turns out, Joe's problem lay in his narrow understanding of the action he had considered taking in order to decide – a definition that consigned him to an insolvable indecision. In actuality, flipping a coin to decide whether to chow down on a Big Mac or a Whopper is not an irrational act at all. In truth, it is *non-rational*, and therefore a completely acceptable means of solving Joe's hunger problems. Using chance as his arbiter does not break his vow to avoid being irrational. Needless to say, there are many more pressing issues that rest on the appropriate definition of terms, such as determining exactly what is meant by an "enemy combatant", a "terrorist", a "fetus", or even a "U.S. citizen," let along determining the essential meaning of the good, the bad, or the beautiful.

Similarly, while many people in our country today argue passionately about justice, liberty, human rights, and so on, we might ask what exactly is meant by these concepts? Are we really disagreeing over fundamental principles in human society, or are we simply talking past each other? If we are unwilling to define these terms and agree on their meaning, is it even possible for us to address the same concern at the same time? For a conscientious scientist or philosopher, the answer is a definite "No way!" In science, if an object is not defined, it does not exist: no definition, and there's really nothing to talk about, or, at best, nothing but pure speculation. What most of us claim to know about ourselves and the world seems to be an amalgamation of opinions and beliefs that we slowly stitch together into some acceptable pattern, a worldview with which we feel most comfortable.

Compounding the knowledge problem, psychologists now inform us that around 65% of verbal communications are misunderstood. We don't seem to realize our arguments are rarely on point, and that we may be talking about two or possibly more, different things at the same time. We unconsciously conflate and thereby confuse issues we are addressing. We believe that the other person knows perfectly well what we mean by justice, liberty, beauty, or what is good, or moral or right. The fact is that few of us have taken the time and effort to determine what we understand by these concepts. Rather than assume that there is mutual understanding of the terms we use when speaking to one another, we would be much better served to assume the opposite.

As explained earlier, Plato and the epistemologists who followed him claimed that we must discriminate between opinions, beliefs and actual *knowledge*. A lucky guess, though sometimes correct, just won't do and does not make the grade. Thus Plato would insist that Henry's conclusion in the thought experiment above was not knowledge in the strict sense of the word. Why? It appears that he can offer no justification for the choice he made. We could argue, however, that his judgment was determined by simply seeing the real barn in the distance and that his visual experience was indeed sufficient justification for his conclusion which, as it turns out, was also true. If we believe what our sense fields tell us and that "seeing is believing"—that a barn is present, in this instance – then this must qualify as more than a lucky guess. Henry wasn't simply following a hunch; he was reporting on his perceptual experience. This in itself should qualify as knowledge, since few of us would survive a day without relying on the information our senses provide.

This thought experiment was actually intended to illustrate how

MITCHELL J. FRANGADAKIS

Plato was *wrong* in his definition of knowledge as a justified, true belief. Wasn't Henry justified in choosing the actual barn that he did, and wasn't his choice correct, i.e. true? Doesn't this fulfill Plato's definition of knowledge? Nonetheless, Plato would disagree with this critique. If Henry were put through the same episode once more, he is much more likely to choose wrong the second time…and the third. The problem is that his method of justification is not systematic. Plato offered geometry and mathematics as examples of systematic knowledge (episteme), and I believe that most of us would agree that today's science qualifies as a systematic justification of beliefs, and, if those beliefs are confirmed as true, as knowledge.

Similar questions regarding knowledge, truth and the veracity of our perceptions also arise when we discuss religious truths. Therefore it would be useful to define unequivocally what we mean by the word *religion*. This invites the further question: Is it even possible to offer a precise definition of this word in the same way that we might define a triangle as a three-sided closed polygon whose interior angles add up to 180 degrees? Keeping all of this in mind, let's try to pin down the concept of religion with a little more precision.

Below are a few definitions to consider:

1) "Yes. We believe in a god and in a supernatural origin of the cosmos – and that by doing Scientology, we can regain our direct awareness of the ultimate truths of things for ourselves." – *Scientology priest*

2) "(Religion is) the belief that there is an unseen order, and that our supreme good lies in harmoniously adjusting ourselves thereto." – *William James, American philosopher*

3) "Religion is a conceptual system that provides an interpretation of the world and the place of humans in it, bases an account of how life should be lived given that interpretation, and expresses this interpretation and lifestyle

in a set of rituals, institutions, and practices." – *Keith Yandel, Philosopher of Religion*

4) "A religion is a system of symbols which acts to establish powerful, pervasive, and long-lasting moods and motivations in men by formulating conceptions of a general order of existence and clothing these conceptions with such an aura of factuality that the moods and motivations seem uniquely realistic." – *Clifford Geert, Anthropologist*

5) "Religion is an illusion and it derives its strength from the fact that it falls in with our instinctual desires." – *Sigmund Freud*

6) "Religion is the means by which humans in every culture define their place in the physical, social and spiritual cosmos even as they make the unobservable and inexplicable reasonable. It is the expression of their worldview." – *Professors Ernest Ettlich and Prakash Chenjeri*

And of course, one of the most well-known definitions of religion from the political philosopher Karl Marx (1818-1883):

7) "Religion is the sigh of the oppressed creature, the heart of a heartless world, and the soul of soulless conditions. It is the opium of the people."

And we should also keep in mind that religion is most often a welcome home to the Unicorns that we are examining.

Given that Socrates was executed for not believing in the gods of ancient Greece (heresy) but nevertheless claimed that he counseled with his personal Daemon (deity) whenever pressed with a momentous decision, we might find it difficult to determine which, if any, of the above definitions he would accept as his own. And of course, this is one of the defining problems of religion: defining religion. I would add to the list above that, whenever an organization provides us with its members to preside over births, weddings, funerals and the salvation of our souls, then we are talking about "religion".

Some people claim they are *spiritual,* but not necessarily religious. A large percentage of Christians in our country claim to believe in God, or some other-worldly reality, but they no longer believe in the religion of the Church per se. In the view of some Catholics, the Pope can proclaim edict after edict regarding birth control, homosexuality, the necessity of sexual abstinence before marriage and so on, but he is not viewed through the same medieval perspective as in times past. In this sense he is no longer infallible, an adjustment in attitude that happened not long after Nietzsche announced, "God is dead." It seems likely then, that those people who label themselves as spiritual do believe in transcendental realities, but they don't make it to Holy Communion or confession all that often.

There are many ways we can interpret what it means to be spiritual as opposed to religious. The psychiatrist, M. Scott Peck (1936-2005) who wrote the popular book, *The Road Less Traveled*, proposed four stages of human spiritual development.

Stage I: This is the elementary stage of development. Individuals in Stage I tend to defy and disobey authority and are unwilling to accept a *will greater than their own*. They are extremely egoistic and lack empathy for others (Picture a three-year old child).

Stage II is the stage of blind obedience to authority figures, and the world is essentially viewed in black and white, good and evil, right and wrong, etc. Many religious people are essentially Stage II people. They have "blind faith" in the higher authority of God. With this model of faith comes a sense of humility and a willingness to obey and serve. The majority of good, law-abiding citizens never move out of Stage II.

Stage III marks the development of higher-order reasoning, including scientific skepticism and persistent questioning. At this stage claims are accepted only if reasonably convincing. Hume was pointing to this stage when he once asked: What is more likely: That a man has arisen from the dead (think of the story of Lazarus), or that the story is wrong? In stage III, the latter conclusion has to be the case.

Stage IV is the mystic's stage, where one begins to appreciate the beauty and mystery of existence. This is different from stage II in that blind faith or acceptance of a belief system out of fear is overcome. The division between self and others slackens, or disappears entirely. Forgiveness and compassion are the fundamental attributes of an individual at this stage.

Peck claimed that each stage marks a significant change in an individual's personality, and his analysis very much mirrors the research done in moral development by the psychologists Kohlberg (1927-1987) and Gilligan (1936-). In Buddhism, the spiritual development described above would aptly fit what is called the cultivation of *relative* and *absolute* Bodhicitta, with Stage IV representing the culmination of one's efforts. More specifically, relative truth in Buddhism is dependent on rational thought, such as knowing that the earth is a globe and not a flat tabletop, whereas one must actually *be* the absolute Truth.

The absolute Truth, as explained in Buddhism, is achieved via "The Middle Way," (analogous in many ways to Aristotle's "Golden Mean"), splitting the difference, as it were, between correlated concepts. Thus:

"'Everything exists: That is one extreme. Everything doesn't exist: That is a second extreme. Avoiding these two extremes, the Tathagata teaches the Dharma via the middle path...'" Buddhist Scripture

It should be pointed out that in the mystical traditions, belief in religious doctrines is often abandoned; those convictions are mere words pointing in the direction of truth, but are not the full actualization of Truth itself. As the Zen saying intones: The moon's reflection in the water should not be mistaken for the moon itself. We have already noted that Universal Reality is called by different names in different religious orders: for example, God or Allah in our monotheistic traditions and Dharmakaya (Truth Body) in Mahayana Buddhism. From the mystic's ground, these names are merely vaporous concepts in contrast to their actual realization.

Philosophers tend to discriminate all religions into two distinct camps, *Real* and *Non-Real*, such that, if we examine the above definitions, we can easily divide them into these two fundamental categories. Realism speaks directly to a supernatural reality, an Ultimate Reality that supersedes mere sense experiences; it is (more often than not) beyond time and space. The non-real view, on the other hand, addresses religion from a primarily emotional, psychological, and/or social perspective, as a means of fulfilling human needs. From this perspective even false beliefs can satisfy those needs. The definitions of religion offered by Marx and Freud obviously fall into the non-real category, whereas the definitions of the Scientologists and William James fall into the realist's camp.

So we return to the fundamental difference between philosophy and religion as referenced earlier: Religion is essentially mythic in that it points to a supernatural reality beyond our normal experiences of space/time, whereas the thrust of philosophy has been to understand the natural realm through observation, analysis, and research in space/time. For philosophy, nature indeed possesses secrets, but they are not invisible gods or supernatural forces. Instead they are obscured principles that explain our existence, and it is up to the natural philosophers and mathematicians to uncover them. For the ancient Greeks, the term for this most elementary principle in nature was the Arche' (as in *archetype*), and the effects from this principle were referred to as the Logos – the natural order that pervades space and time.

The pre-Socratic philosopher Thales was fully aware of the prevalent myths and religious orders of ancient Greece, but spoke instead of natural elements – specifically of water – as the source of all that exists. For natural philosophers, supernatural accounts simply testify to a lack of understanding, or even deleterious trips into the various realms of superstitious beliefs. Religions merely epitomize

THE UNICORN PROBLEM

humanity's ignorance regarding the true cause of things. When a religious adept speaks of natural events or even miracles as though they were transcendental in origin, the natural philosopher calls this superstition. It is not all that surprising therefore, that there still remains a sharp division—even hostility at times—between religious doctrines and scientific reasoning, as well as between religious doctrines and philosophy.

The philosopher Bertrand Russell offers a story that illustrates the difficulty and depth of the problem. At the time of the so-called "Black Death" plague, in scale the worst epidemic humankind has ever experienced, the pastor of a small congregation was growing worried about the contamination reaching the people of his village. It was known that large numbers of the population in a nearby province had already been infected and were dying in a horrible manner from this deadly disease. Therefore the pastor reasoned that this awful reality couldn't be far from their doorsteps. In light of this, he decided that the best recourse was to call his congregation together so that they might all pray to God for deliverance from this evil. The true believers came together in the small crowded Church and called to God for help. Because of their trust in the efficacy of their prayers and their ignorance regarding the etiology of the disease, every member of that congregation, along with the priest, died from the plague within a few days' time.

***

There is another means by which religion judges Truth and Knowledge – wisdom both timeless and universal – and that is through the testimonies of prophets, mystics, and other creative souls who claim to have had a life-changing Religious Experience (R.E.). There are abundant examples in the New Testament where we are told, for instance, about Saul of Tarsus, a Jewish lawyer who, as a young man on his way to Damascus to continue his persecution of Christians, has an extraordinary revelation that leads to his conversion as St. Paul. Jesus himself was led by the Holy Spirit to wander alone in the desert, ultimately to be tempted by the Devil, but whose steadfast belief in the Scriptures released him from that evil personage. We also read that Shakyamuni Gautama becomes the Buddha after his revelation—his personal liberation from cyclic existence—under the Bodhi tree (a large fig tree), a liberation accomplished after years of exhausting yogic and meditative practices. And there is Mohammed, sequestered in his cave, entertaining repeated visions of the Angel Gabriel, thereby receiving the sacred transmissions we now call the Koran. Tibetan Buddhists claim that their Tulkus (Conscious Incarnates) are able to reveal hidden "Mind Treasures" (Termas), and Vajrayana practitioners revere these as revealed Truth.

Mother Theresa offers us the following description of her Religious Experience: "...I was at prayer on a festival of the glorious Saint Peter when I saw Christ at my side—or, to put it better, I was conscious of Him, for neither with the eyes of the body nor with those of the soul did I see anything. I thought He was quite close to me and I saw that it was He Who, as I thought, was speaking to me. Being completely ignorant that visions of this kind could occur, I was at first very much afraid, and did nothing but weep, though, as soon as He addressed a single word to me to reassure me, I became quiet again, as I had been before, and was quite happy and free from fear...He was at my right hand, and a witness of everything that I was doing, and that, whenever I became slightly recollected or was not greatly distracted, I could not but be aware of His nearness to me."

Narratives describing transformative experiences such as this have been passed to us by previous generations for well over two thousand years, and they provide the core of what is deemed Revealed Truth. Revealed Truth is believed to be the voice of the divine. Similar stories abound in all the major religions. All religions are grounded in the mystical experiences of their founders.

But what is the Religious Experience, and is it the same or different from a mystical experience? Is an insight that I might have, such as the interconnected nature of all existence that suddenly

THE UNICORN PROBLEM

appears obvious to me while planting tomatoes in my garden... might this be called a Religious Experience (R.E.)? What if that specific insight changed my whole view of life? Or does the R.E. have to be something far more profound, a vision, or an epiphany (literally, a *call from beyond*), or the overwhelming sense that God or Buddha Mind is present within me? What do these terms mean, or since they are so highly personal, do they remain beyond translation into the general language system?

As for the R.E. in Buddhism, the conceptual explanation of that experience, no matter how profound its content, is deemed a relative truth. It is deemed the best approximation of truth possible through language. If one has a desire to know the Absolute Truth, this must be done through personal mind training and yoga. In this way, one knows the Absolute Truth in much the same manner that one knows he or she is a member of the human race on planet earth: common sense in result, but intuition as the means or cause.

According to the philosopher Ludwig Wittgenstein (1889-1951), language operates by certain rules (a revision of his earlier pictorial explanation of language) and that the established rules of the religious language-game are a bad fit with the language rules of science, or even those of general philosophy. In the same way that a logical positivist can easily dismiss religious claims—if so inclined—so, too, can a person of faith dismiss the so-called Laws of science. Why? Because their language systems play by a different set of rules: religious followers and scientists play different language games. It would be like putting a baseball team and a football team on the field at the same time, and then crying, "Play Ball!" No game would happen, just chaos. All the baseball players would be playing by their set of rules while simultaneously breaking every rule in the football players' book—and vice-versa.

Apart from formal doctrine, there is nothing solid that we can rest on when explaining religious language; the meaning and import of religious concepts remains ambiguous or equivocal—despite the cries of the literalists in the congregation. Religious language, and especially the language used when trying to describe the R.E., necessarily resorts to analogies, metaphors, and paradoxes when discussing a realm that may in fact eclipse temporal and spatial realms altogether. Religion, as does science, speaks its own language. If the Zen Buddhist Suzuki Roshi claims that his little mind has melded with Big Mind, a tape measure isn't going to do us much good. Nonetheless, there have been countless attempts to bridge this translation gap.

There are numerous accounts of different types of R.E.'s. Some are exclusive and private, such as that of Mother Theresa's, an experience transcending sensory impressions. Other accounts of R.E.'s are collective in nature, such as the accounts of a communal vision in Lourdes, France, that was witnessed (according to accounts) by hundreds of people simultaneously. A R.E. in Buddhism might be labeled as "…beyond the beyond," a *direct cognition* that is more a type of intuitive knowing than sensorial. This type of experience is generally considered more real than a vision, or any other kind of sense-based experience. Sense impressions, including mystical visions, may come and go, but Buddha Mind is constant and Immutable. This kind of Buddhist R.E. is an immersion into the Wholeness of things, and this Wholeness is oftentimes described as Timeless and Universal. Using Suzuki's language again, a Buddhist Satori or Kensho is an experience wherein one's little mind becomes One with the Big Mind (God or Buddha Mind). This Big Mind is not actually bigger in the usual sense of that word, but rather means essential Mind; Big Mind, it is maintained, is our essence, our true nature.

I prefer to skip the word *religious* altogether and speak more directly to *mystical* experiences. By that I mean that the core explanation for these experiences, whether sense-based or not, is transcendental—they are not based on what we normally refer to as natural phenomena. Normal perceptions are eclipsed in some fashion. No principles of physics can explain Mother Theresa's story, her attempt to put into words an experience that no matrix of space and time can encapsulate. Her level of certainty, her confidence in the absolute Truth of her experience, overrides all empirical

THE UNICORN PROBLEM

evidence. Indeed, some psychiatrists might explain away her experience as some kind of psychotic break.

The psychologist Abraham Maslow states: "The very beginning, the intrinsic core, the essence, the universal nucleus of every known high religion (unless Confucianism is also called a religion) has been the private, lonely, personal illumination, revelation, or ecstasy of some acutely sensitive prophet or seer. The high religions call themselves revealed religions and each of them tends to rest its validity, its function, and its right to exist on the codification and the communication of this original mystic experience or revelation from the lonely prophet to the mass of human beings in general."

The other problem involved with defining religious experiences is the word *religious* itself. What does it mean? We've already seen the difficulty in pinning down any *one* meaning for the word *religion,* so to address religious experiences simply complicates the matter. Is the content of what we refer to as a religious experience necessarily religious in nature? For example, some would argue that, of course Mother Theresa believed it was Jesus speaking to her. She was a Christian, after all. She merely put what she couldn't understand into a culturally defined language system that she could grasp. If she were a Muslim, she might have claimed it was Mohammad or Allah that spoke to her, not Jesus.

Still another difficulty with categorizing these experiences as religious is that they very often have little or nothing to do with religious doctrine per se. Oftentimes these extraordinary experiences can occur to individuals not associated with any religion. Nikos Kazantzakis, quoted at the beginning of this chapter, was a philosopher, writer and mystic. He was eventually accused of heresy, and excommunicated from the Greek Orthodox Church. Gurdjieff was also a mystic, and he based his teachings on various philosophical examinations more so than ancient religious traditions. Additionally, the novelist Aldous Huxley was a mystic. All of these men based their lives, and particularly their moral views, on interior experiences that were far removed from normal day-to-day experiences, especially those experiences associated with Imams, Rabbis, crosses, or sacred books.

Russell puts it this way: "The mystic insight begins with the sense of a mystery unveiled, of a hidden wisdom now suddenly become certain beyond the possibility of a doubt. The sense of certainty and revelation comes earlier than any definite belief. The definite beliefs at which mystics arrive are the result of reflection upon the inarticulate experience gained in the moment of insight."

Oftentimes the mystical experience can be overwhelming, providing a vivid meaning to the word *awesome*, i.e., full of awe (awful). Huxley describes the awfulness of the *mysterium tremendum* in his book *The Doors of Perception*.

He offers this explanation of the experience in the following way: "The literature of religious experience abounds in references to the pains and terrors overwhelming those who have come, too suddenly, face to face with some manifestation of the *Mysterium Tremendum*. In theological language, this fear is due to the incompatibility between man's egotism and the divine purity, between man's self-aggravated Separateness and the infinity of God."

One thing we can agree on is that if a religious experience takes place, it seems that its final explanation necessarily rests on a supernatural source for that experience, and more often than not, this source is deemed Sacred or Divine. This could be the God of Christianity, the Allah of Islam, or a direct cognition of the Dharmakaya in Buddhism. It is unavailable to the ordinary mind of humanity; it rests beyond the scope of the normal sense fields, and ultimately remains non-conceptual and ineffable. This is shared by all of the major religions: the-intrinsic rejection of an earth-based reality for something deemed superior – the immutable nature of the Absolute Truth of Buddhism and the Necessary Existence of the Perfect Creator of Judaism, Christianity, and Islam. Philo (20 B.C.-50 A.D.), a Jewish Hellenistic philosopher from Alexandria, said that God was not similar in any conceptual manner to heaven, our world, or human beings: he has no name, cannot be perceived, remains eternally self-sufficient and immutable (Greek: ἑαυτῷ ἱκανός).

THE UNICORN PROBLEM

The thorny difficulty that each religion must explain away is why these compelling metaphysical views don't necessarily agree with one another, and oftentimes contradict one another. If two religions disagree over why there is something rather than nothing, for instance, or what constitutes a truly righteous and good life, then one of them has to be wrong. And it just as easily could be that they are both wrong. As a consequence, each religion becomes an exclusive club, and nonbelievers or those without sufficient faith are requested to wait in the vestibule. This promise of transcendental forces that offer human beings absolute Truth and Reality makes all religions susceptible to doubt, criticism, and ultimately, rejection by people who claim to be guided by the light of reason alone. The absence of a sufficient justification for these kinds of metaphysical claims – reasons that compel our assent and are therefore accepted as true – is the essential Unicorn Problem common to all religious doctrines.

What we refer to as Eastern religions, and Buddhism in particular, base the ultimate truth of their claims regarding Reality and the nature of existence directly on a mystical experience. Indeed, the Saints, Prophets, Gurus, and Yogis of all religious traditions affirm the Truth of their particular doctrines through reports of their own unique supernatural experiences. This is the basis of all revealed theologies. Although Buddhism advances countless sophisticated arguments to substantiate its doctrine, the heart of all proofs lies within the Buddhist practitioners themselves. Truth is within, not without. Looking out is merely peering more deeply into the darkness of Plato's Cave. Reality must be intuited or revealed, not reasoned. In this sense, absolute Truth is *for oneself only*. One is either free from the wear and tear of cyclic existence or not. One is either realized or not; one is either liberated or not...assuming that liberation or salvation is even necessary or possible. It cannot be both ways at once...can it?

***

MITCHELL J. FRANGADAKIS

We have returned to our basic epistemological issue, that big Unicorn in the sky: How do we determine if a claim is true, regardless of whether that claim is scientific, religious, mystical or otherwise? What constitutes a truth-bearing claim that cannot possibly be false? This absence of complete certainty or even a viable method of obtaining certainty is the essence of the problem we encounter when trying to saddle Unicorns.

Religions offer various arguments to substantiate their positions, and those positions, as already mentioned, fall into the same general categories as we see in traditional Western philosophy: metaphysics, ontology, logic, ethics and so on. Hence there are the ontological, cosmological, teleological, and moral arguments proposed by Christian theologians. The central premise, for example, of the Christian moral argument is that without religious beliefs there can be no foundational justification for moral conduct. Without God we would all run the risk of living a life of sin, lost and without any trustworthy moral guidance in our lives (Some critics might argue otherwise, claiming it is precisely *because* of religion that moral conduct has run amok). In Buddhism, Karma serves the same purpose of justifying the moral doctrine. Where is *right action* and *wrong action* without the idea of Karma? If we reject this argument, then what does serve as foundational justification for moral principles – if anything? Traditionally, we insist that a claim is true based on certain premises.

According to the Stanford Encyclopedia of Philosophy, we have the following sources for knowledge and justification in our Western epistemological traditions:

Perception

Introspection

Memory

Reason

Testimony

THE UNICORN PROBLEM

To which I would add: Authority and Tradition, which might include aspects of all of the above.

It isn't in the scope of this text to specifically define each of these terms. In one way their meanings are self-evident and, in another way, they have very specific connotations within our philosophical and psychological traditions. The terms *perception* and *introspection*, for example, have evolved through various definitions over the centuries, based in large part upon the expanded understanding of our natural world and human biology. These terms mean quite different things when we shift them from their scientific or psychological context to the religious context of mystical (religious) experiences.

"One family of epistemological issues about perception arises when we concern ourselves with the psychological nature of the perceptual processes through which we acquire knowledge of external objects. According to *direct realism*, we can acquire such knowledge because we can directly perceive such objects. For example, when you see a tomato on the table, *what you perceive* is the tomato itself. According to *indirect realism*, we acquire knowledge of external objects by virtue of perceiving something else, namely appearances or sense data. An *indirect realist* would say that, when you see and thus know that there is a tomato on the table, what you really see is not the tomato itself but a *tomato-like sense-datum* or some such entity." – S.E.P.

So if we return to Plato's argument that knowledge requires our beliefs to be both justified and true a (justified, true belief, or JTB), and that this process of justification must be done in a systematic fashion, what happens when we require Plato to justify his claim? How is the claim that all knowledge must be true and justifiable, as well as systematic, demonstrated to be true? We end up with the "up-and-over" mental flips that self-referencing arguments always produce.

A classic example of a self-referencing argument is the Liar's

Paradox: If I say that everything I say to you is a lie, am I lying or telling you the truth? If you give it a moment's thought, you'll see that there is no answer; it is paradoxical in that any answer contradicts the primary premise. Another example, mentioned earlier in this text, is Socrates' retort to the Sophist's argument when Protagoras (490-420), spokesperson for the Sophists, argued that "… man is the measure of all things, of things that are, that they are, of things that are not, that they are not…."

If all truth is relative to humankind, Socrates asked, is that relatively true or absolutely true? By definition, according to the Sophists, there is no absolute truth. If they claimed that their position was absolute, they would be contradicting themselves, given that the argument would then be that it is absolutely true that all truth is relative. Given these logical dilemmas, are we then doomed to be epistemological agnostics, and deny that truth exists at all? For example, the radical skeptic Pyrrho (360-270 B.C.E.) required constant attention by his followers. The reason? He was dismissive of all beliefs, including the beliefs that fire is hot and gravity makes falling dangerous. As a consequence, he had a proclivity for walking through campfires or towards the edge of cliffs (so goes the story, anyway).

Don't all systems of knowledge, relative or absolute, necessarily rest on one or more general assumptions? Or perhaps I should simply decide that my Truth, which is probably distinct from your Truth, requires no justification, no reason for being the absolute fact that it is. In effect, facts become nothing more than what I believe, and facts for you are what you believe.

***

Scientific knowledge must begin with assumptions, if only to discern in which direction our inquiries should begin. Sometimes these assumptions are called axioms, postulates, or even self-evident truths. They are taken as truth-bearing claims that require no justification. All of this, of course, creates a problem: how do we

THE UNICORN PROBLEM

know that these axioms and other self-evident truths are, indeed, True? Why are these particular claims exempt from justification? This was the issue Descartes struggled with in his attempt to discover a foundation for all knowledge, i.e., a Truth about which he could not possibly be wrong. He believed that if you have that kind of certainty upon which to build, the rest of Truth and Knowledge follows necessarily through logical demonstrations.

During recent political campaigns (sometimes referred to as "poop-throwing parties") there have been animated arguments over what constitutes a *fact*. Some philosophers might agree with the radical skeptics on this issue and claim that ultimately, *there are no facts*. They might argue, like the Earth Giants in Plato's allegory, that what we call facts are construed truths, not ultimate, unquestionable Truth. But that is arguing over facts in a philosophical and epistemological sense, not the ordinary or relative realm of knowledge in which politics participates. If I say that the current President of the U.S. is Barack Obama, or that a ruler is 12 inches long or that Elvis Presley is dead, these are undeniable facts about the everyday world in which we all live. This is all information worthy of belief, both true and justified.

We now have online "fact-checkers" who determine which of the so-called facts proffered by politicians are in fact true, and which are misrepresentations or outright fabrications. This issue was addressed recently on a TV show, and one of the political pundits took umbrage with the entire process of checking facts. He asked, as though perplexed: "Who is going to check the fact-checkers?" To which we might add: Who is going to check the facts of the fact-checkers who check the facts of the fact-checkers? If this process is not to go on forever, we must have fact-checkers that we trust (we call them "experts") to put an end to it all. Without this final fact-checking station, we are left with examples of the infinite regress problem, bringing into focus yet another herd of unicorns on the horizon.

Aristotle and later philosophers answered this general epistemological problem by insisting that we have to begin somewhere. If we doubt the truth of any and all assumptions (self-evident truths, axioms, etc.), then no true conclusions could possibly follow. Notwithstanding his theory of *Four Causes*, Aristotle began his own epistemology with ten basic categories of understanding, including such concepts as substance, quantity, quality, relations, and so on. This became a blueprint for human knowledge that has been followed by countless philosophers, and by contemporary science. What these categories offer, when coupled with Aristotle's four laws of logic, is a place to initiate our search for knowledge, concepts and rational operations of the mind, by which we can organize and understand our world. Immanuel Kant would later reprise this same idea, claiming that the human mind possesses a self-activity, and that our minds necessarily participate in the process of piecing together an understandable world. The human mind is a not the *tabula rasa* that Locke claimed. As mentioned previously, space and time were for Kant the necessary forms or templates (his "transcendental intuitions") for comprehending our world. We cannot conceive of anything absent of the concepts of time and space. Without the ideas of space and time the world cannot exist–at least not for us. Ultimately, if we were to doubt the truth of any and all concepts or categories, i.e., if no assumptions are allowed, then no knowledge is possible. The infinite regress—facts checking facts checking facts—must have a cut-off point.

  Let me offer an example of a possible alternative to this logical predicament from the point of view of a philosophical camp known as the Reformed Epistemologists. Plantinga, an elegant spokesperson for this group, offers an alternative to Plato's epistemological position. He begins by mentioning what is referred to in philosophy as the *problem of other minds*. How do I know, he asks, that my internal experience of consciousness is also the same kind of experience that you are having? How do I know that you have a mind that senses and knows in the same way mine does? My mind is a private experience, as is yours. Where's the bridge, other than a logical inference?

  Plantinga argues that there is no reasonable proof possible for this claim that minds, other than my own, exist. It is a belief that

THE UNICORN PROBLEM

cannot be reasonably justified. It is intellectually indeterminable – another order of Unicorns – and completely dependent on inductive reasoning based upon inferences made from physical observations. This belief that you possess a consciousness in the same sense that I experience being conscious qualifies as knowledg*e* for Plantinga despite Plato's admonitions. Even if it is not possible to satisfy Plato's criteria for a belief to be called knowledge, Plantinga is claiming that knowledge is nonetheless possible. The PBB of the reformed epistemologists snatches the same goodies as Plato's JTB, but in a different way.

In further defense of this knowledge reformation, Plantinga reminds us of the thought experiment introduced by B. Russell: "How do we know that the universe didn't all begin 10 minutes ago?"

Before you immediately dismiss what appears to be a silly question...think about it. Upon serious reflection we find that this is not easy to answer. In fact, we can't answer it sufficiently. It remains intellectually indeterminable if we will only be satisfied with an absolutely true and certain conclusion. What we can say with a great deal of confidence is that the odds are very much against it.

Therefore, according to Plantinga, our belief that the universe didn't really begin 10 minutes ago does not entirely fit Plato's definition of knowledge. Rather it is once again a PBB, a reformed notion of knowledge. It is from these types of premises that Plantinga leaps to the conclusion that a Christians belief in God is also a PBB. Properly speaking then, we can actually have knowledge of God's existence through our belief in Him.

The problem that consistently steps to the front is the method by which we should justify our judgments, beliefs, and claims about what is true and what is not, what is right and what is wrong, how we should live our lives and what we should avoid. This is yet again the problem with Unicorns, and this particular herd leaps directly into the breach between faith and reason.

Perhaps faith in the common sense of the word is not appropriate here, since I am considering how I know that the sun will rise in the East tomorrow—apart from the fact that it doesn't rise at all and is an illusion created by the earth's rotation relative to the sun. The fact is I don't really know this; I simply have a strong conviction that Mother Nature will remain steadfast and provide in her usual ways, with tomorrow's Sol so similar to yesterday's that I won't notice the difference. In other words, I only have the belief that tomorrow will come, but the certain knowledge of that fact eludes me until tomorrow actually arrives. Scientists offer us a system of justification through their strong belief in the uniformity of nature, but even this leaves a measure of uncertainty.

Hume pointed out that there is nothing in the definition of the past and in the definition of the future that links the two together in a necessary conjunction, or what we call a causal relationship. The notion of causation is a sophisticated method of forecasting future events (certainly more sophisticated than reading tea leaves) based on the belief that how nature worked in the past will necessarily hold true in the future. In a causal relationship, whenever "X" occurs, "Y" must follow. This is the belief. And cause and effect relationships form the conceptual bedrock in modern science. So imagine that I witness a white cue-ball roll on the green felt pool table and strike a black eight ball. In analyzing what I have just seen – and holding fast to my empiricist's principles by drawing conclusions only from the evidence provided by my sense fields – what is it that I know I have witnessed? What I would be inclined to say is that I know that when the white ball struck the black ball, the white ball *caused* the formerly stationary ball to move. And Hume replies: Show me this cause.

If we remain true to empiricism, we must admit that this concept of causation is inferred, but not perceived. I perceive one ball moving, then the next, but I never witness anything called a "cause." In a like fashion, John Locke, one of the founding fathers of the modern empirical camp in philosophy, was forced to admit that we never really perceive matter or the actual *substance* of things, either. What we do see is the power of matter, i.e., its effect on our sense organs. Properly speaking, the concept of matter is a metaphysical term, not empirical, similar in that sense to the metaphysical concept of God. Matter is not demonstrable through empirical evidence in

THE UNICORN PROBLEM

the same way that a cause is never experienced: we witness only a simple contiguity of events. All that our experience tells us is that one event follows another with no actual cause (or matter) in sight. In his final analysis Hume maintained that, in principle, anything could be the cause of anything.

CHAPTER 8
IS NOTHING SACRED?

"The Divine is not this and it is not that."
Vedic Aphorism

"In his *Principia Mathematica* Newton provided a wonderful example showing how the moon is kept in its orbit in just the same way as an object falls to the earth. He illustrated this by means of a cannon shooting a cannon ball further and further. In the limit, the earth curves away as fast as the ball falls, with the eventual result being that the cannon ball will return to the spot where it was fired, and, if not impeded, will go around again and again. This is what the moon is doing. We could arrive at the same conclusion through calculation. But Newton's thought experiment provides that elusive understanding. It's a wonderful example of the 'aha effect'."
S.E.P.

RIDING UNICORNS

Consulting the ancient Vedic scriptures of the religious traditions of India, we find the story of Agni, known as the God of Fire, the oldest son of Brahman and one of the most celebrated of deities in that tradition. He is variously described as an odd creature (i.e., with two or three heads, several legs, a thousand eyes, etc.), but always he is associated with fire — flames radiate from his body, the shamanistic instruments that he holds are made of flames, etc. Much like Prometheus in the ancient Greek myths, this is the God who created the sun and stars and who bestows immortality on his worshipers. He is the internal force of the universe, consuming all so that new growth is possible, like a forest fire clearing the soil for seedlings that lie in wait. The universe is, figuratively speaking, on fire, and Agni is the ignition. All is ultimately sacrificed to his flames.

Fire has also been a consistent symbol of spiritual purification and enlightenment, with examples in mythology and both ancient and modern religions from around the world. The ancient Upanishad informs us that the essence of man and that of the sun are one and the same. In the Fire Sermon given by the Buddha (*Āditta-pariyāya*), he tells the assembled monks that all phenomena, including consciousness, is on fire with flames of passion, aversion, and delusion.

In the Tibetan Buddhist Vajrayana tradition, enlightened beings are oftentimes depicted surrounded by a "wisdom fire", symbolizing the transformation of ego-attachment into liberation. Flames spread outward, like intense halos that surround every aspect of an enlightened being, similar to the coronas displayed in Christian iconography. Radiance is the key, an attribute of the awakened soul. The process of awakening, of the realization of our essential nature, is coeval with the spontaneous arising of all phenomena; and that spontaneity is like fire itself, consuming all in its path.

All of the primary elements exhibit this intrinsic creative force: the evening winds whip through open fields with serpentine pulses pushing through reeds and flowers. What they might do next remains unpredictable. The turbulence of a stream as it yields to the rocks along its course is beyond mathematical calculations. No conceptual scheme can absolutely predict the next move of the eternal flux, the next leap of the flame or spiraling flow of the current. Yet the metaphor of the elements, and fire in particular, also points to the inherent illumination and beauty within all that exists – a spontaneous arising, and also for the ancient Greeks, a demonstration of the sacred Logos, that intrinsic order that upholds our very world. And by some miraculous ability of the human psyche, we are able to grasp this essential nature. Paraphrasing Einstein, we might say that the greatest mystery of the universe is that we are able to understand it.

In commenting on the Greek philosophical school of Stoicism, Professor Bewkes states: "The beneficent universal law, called Providence, God, Logos, or Divine Fire is itself rational. This divine fire which pervades the universe is of the same stuff as the sparks which light the rational souls of men. ..."

The pre-Socratic philosopher Heraclitus came to similar conclusions when describing the animating force of the Cosmos: all is in motion, everything is in flux – it is not possible to step into the same river twice, or hold fast to any moment. Every passing instant dissolves into eternity. When Heraclitus reached for an appropriate metaphor for this shape-shifting reality in which we find ourselves, he spoke as a voice of Agni…he spoke of Universal Fire. The Fire of Heraclitus was the underlying flux itself, the fundamental attribute of all that exists, what we might call the foundational substance or essence of Reality. For Heraclitus, this was the cause of change and motion, or more accurately, it was the *very nature* of change and motion. And, like our world, it remained fixed with the paradoxical attributes of both order and unpredictability. Heraclitus was asking us to embrace the implicit Reason (Logos) within this flux, while simultaneously dismissing any conceptual renderings of existence. Why? Because all concepts are laden with values; all concepts are interpretations of Reality, and, thereby, in various degrees of separation from what is True. Be reasonable, but don't forget to override logical constructs regarding Truth and knowledge; determining their actual meanings is not obtainable in this way.

In his wonderfully intriguing book, *Why Does the World Exist?*, Jim Holt, scientific writer for both the *New Yorker Magazine* and the *New York Times*, writes: "The temporal finitude of our universe – here today (but not yesterday), gone tomorrow – makes its existence seem all the more insecure and contingent. And mysterious. A world with solid ontological foundations, it seems, just wouldn't behave like this. It would exist eternally and imperishably. Such a world, unlike the finite Big Bang universe, would have an aura of self-sufficiency. It might even harbor the cause of its own being."

Heraclitus argued that Being is an illusion. There exists only Becoming. Like traditional Zen masters, he preferred to explain reality through paradox. To capture the essential nature of existence, philosophical concepts were far too stolid, unlike the decidedly effective symbol of fire as the element of continual regeneration and change. Philosophers who advocated the study and analysis of Being, who partitioned the questions of existence into discrete but permanent categories and then compiled rules ordering their relationships, or philosophers more enigmatically inclined, like Thales, who posited water as the original element from which all phenomena arose, were unwittingly propagating foolish ideas. For Heraclitus, the very concept that something *is* – that it has inherent *being* – was a flawed concept, an idea that ignores the mainstay of our experiences. Nothing stands still long enough to have the constancy required to be something. *Impermanence* rules all that exists.

In counterpoint, Parmenides argues that all movement or change is the actual illusion, and that Being is a unified whole that cannot be parceled into bits of time and space. His student Zeno (490-430 BCE) claimed that when an arrow flies through the sky, it cannot possibly be moving: at each moment it must be completely where it is, hence stationary. Every moment that follows must be the same, therefore the arrow never actually moves.

These contradictory claims about Being, Becoming, and even non-Being, abound within our Western philosophical and theological traditions. Time and time again, we find that fundamental ontological problems reduce to an emphasis on either sense experiences or logic (with the help of mathematics) as the passage into Reality and Truth. Logical principles are viewed as unchanging, and therefore appreciated as everlasting and immutable, whereas sense experiences are turgid, a perpetual parade of passing events despite the "laws" that purport to explain them – all phenomena here one moment and gone the next. Which of these two portals to the world should we trust, especially since when taken together, they oftentimes force us into contradictory positions?

Perhaps in an attempt to circumvent these sorts of problems, Buddhism argues that there are two fundamental levels to Truth, two modes so to speak, such that movement and impermanence comprise only one side of truth, that being the *relative* aspect of natural existence. There is another side to the story however, an immutable aspect hidden deep within our everyday experiences. Buddhists believe that through the cessation of desires, the psychological and personal realm – the realm of privileged access—one can realize an inner peace and rest; that an extraordinary sense of unchanging stillness lies in the depth of impermanence, but to reach this epiphany our egos must play dead…at least for the moment. A common aphorism in Buddhist meditative practices is that of water in a pond: if you constantly agitate the water you will never see the bottom. Once stillness or equanimity of mind is achieved, an alternative mode of understanding, a mode of mind closer to that of faith than of reason, reveals itself. In this alternative reality the relative mind, the mind affixed to the habits generated by motion and stimulation, relaxes and eventually dissipates, leaving, as Parmenides suggested, a single source underneath all of our dualistic considerations. But for Buddhist philosophers like Nagarjuna this single source is neither Being nor Non-Being (perhaps closer to Russell's "neutral monism"), yet it remains the realm of Absolute Truth.

Heraclitus spoke directly to the question that faces any reflective soul: Why is there change? Why does everything appear to be in a state of perpetual alteration? For Saint Aquinas, much like Aristotle, movement and change revealed that nature was incomplete, a continuous dissatisfaction with the status quo as all things moved towards the perfection of God. For both Aquinas and Aristotle a fully actualized being—God—is what we most desire to know.

Santayana summarizes this sentiment when he remarks: "…the goal of life is a Separate being, already existing, namely, the mind of God, eternally realizing what the world aspires to." Eschewing this

THE UNICORN PROBLEM

teleological view, contemporary science offers a more objective explanation. Things may be changing continuously, but maybe the change itself is occurring in a predictable manner. Perhaps a mathematical algorithm will explain how change is, in some manner, rational. Perhaps even the paradox is not a paradox in that the shape of change never changes. It is as if the old axiom, "the more things change the more they stay the same", is in concurrence with scientific thinking.

Nonetheless, perhaps we should also heed the words of the Stoic Marcus Aurelius when he noted: "The Universe is change, life is an opinion."

***

If in fact Heraclitus and the Buddhists are correct in saying that phenomena—all appearances — are the very flux of impermanence itself, then what can be said about other abstract ideas like substance, causation, infinity, perfection, or the Good? Is it possible for the universe to sit still long enough for us to name something and study it as though it really was a thing holding still for our inspection? If I examine the cup on my table carefully, I might wonder: does this cup have an essence, an attribute without which it could not be what it is? No philosopher, scientist or theologian has yet satisfactorily answered whether this cup possesses substance, something underneath all the other attributes that I attach to it, something that is unchanging, such as the invisible atoms of Leucippus and Democritus.

Can a concept such as *substance* be justifiably reified? Additionally, can we apply pure concepts to concrete reality? If everything, including the cup before me, is in continuous motion, how can we even begin to define it as substantial and real? Still, we suppose that there must be something constant before us, despite Kant's admonition that substance is only an idea, but not a reality we might experience.

Something must make that cup what it is, and that, according to Aristotle, would be the blending of its form with matter, the hylomorphic substance that – in conjunction with the organization of that substance into a functional form – acts like a bonding agent, holding all of the variable attributes together. Because of this underlying constancy, I could look at my cup in any color, size, texture, weight, etc. and still proclaim it to be a cup. Ultimately, I might add, Aristotle would define the cup through its purpose (*telos*): that which can serve as a cup, is a cup. But if we claim that some cups are better than others because they fulfill their intended function better, then Aristotle would state that a cup (or anything else) that best fulfills its intended purpose is thereby a *virtuous* (excellent) cup.

Extrapolating from Aristotle, St. Aquinas argued that this notion of telos or goal accounted for all of nature's ways, and concluded: "…Now, whatever lacks intelligence cannot move towards an end, unless it be directed by some being endowed with knowledge and intelligence; as the arrow is shot to its mark by the archer. Therefore, some intelligent being exists by whom all natural things are directed to their end; and this being we call *God*."

Thus it seems that the very heart of material stuff is action, an energy-bursting report straight from the eyes of Agni. In Buddhist terms, this ever-moving chain of action is called Karma, the energetic vehicle by which change is transferred from one moment to the next. Like the river of Heraclitus, the physical universe is constantly at play, an inherently creative force that is perpetually on the move. And it is the same with my internal universe. When I stop to pay attention to my internal reality, I find no stability whatsoever. My thoughts are like crackling flames, jumping this way and that. My emotions shift according to circumstance, sensitive to prevailing conditions, coming and going like the winds that feed the fire. My memories change over time, to such an extent that my remembrance of things past is more likely the labor of my imagination than a past reality reproduced. When the philosopher Hume wrote about his search for a Self within, all he found was a fleeting bundle of thoughts and perceptions, no stationary memory, no constant, sustained Self anywhere. And in so many ways, religious views themselves center on the issue of self-identity: Is my soul or essence transcendent of my personality (ego)? Is it my only unchangeable attribute? And will it survive the death of my body? Unlike the Stoics of Athens who sought only peace of mind (*ataraxia*), the golden ring for all religious doctrines, the ultimate reward that every faith promises, is immortality.

On the cosmic scale, we could ask (as did Aristotle) if there is a Prime Mover, an invisible something that propelled the Universe into action in the first place—a Big Bang, perhaps? The Big Bang event has not yet been falsified in the scientific community, and all of the evidence thus far seems to confirm the theory. This however does not mean that it is certainly true, but rather that, so far all the facts seem to fit the conceptual scheme. Still we could ask what banged in the first place. If the Big Bang is the first moment of cosmic existence, the energy or material that exploded must have preceded the explosion itself. As the ethnobotanist Terrence McKenna (1946-2000) remarked: with the Big Bang Theory, scientists are requesting one small miracle, after which they can explain all the rest (which, if you think about it, is pretty impressive).

Buddhists claim that, regardless of how it all began, leaving aside the question as to whether or not there was even a beginning, all of our mundane experiences are merely illusions. The analogy often given for the experience of being alive is that of a dream—of something presently experienced but ultimately unreal. Why is that? Because within our experience, it appears evident that nothing, not one event, is unchanging. Each so-called moment is but an ongoing flux of events, analogous to Heraclitus's river whose flowing waters preclude stepping into the same spot twice. Our belief in tangible, stable, (hence) real things outside or within us, our "self" included, is the core of this illusion. The Zen scholar and philosopher Alan Watts, for example, claimed that there is no such thing as a "noun": when we speak of a cup, for example, what we should actually refer to is a "cupping." The cup is pure action itself, and never the same cup twice. So, this physical life is dream-like in that it is ephemeral, like a flame in an evening wind; or like bubbles bursting on a stream when their Karma – the chain of causes and effects that produced their appearance in the first place – is exhausted.

To call phenomena illusory, as Buddhists are wont to do, doesn't mean that there are no experiences. Even a dream is real in the sense that it occurs. The Sanskrit term *Maya*, which has been popularly translated as *illusion*, originally meant something quite different: the fundamental energy of a Supreme Spirit, similar to the Greek term *Logos* or the Divine Fire of Heraclitus. When a magician pulls a rabbit out of the hat, we also call that an illusion. We call it that because we know that it is magician's trick and not a little miracle of sorts; we know that the physical laws of ordinary reality have not been suspended for our benefit. We realize that the illusion created by a magician is a perceptual anomaly that doesn't literally change reality, but rather simply redirects our attention.

Buddhists have a similar understanding of illusion. I may believe that physical existence, with all of its tangible attributes, such as density and form and quantity, is the only reality available to us. But this is like the magician's trick, an illusion created by the misdirection of my attention onto what is ephemeral, away from what is unchanging. The Hindu snake-rope illusion is another example of this same conundrum: a poor gardener nearly suffers a heart attack because he mistakes a coiled rope for a cobra ready to strike. Most epistemological systems, East and West, conclude that the perception of the snake, since it is grounded in ignorance, is false, whereas once ignorance is removed, the perception of the rope is true. Buddhist epistemology in the Viijnanavadin sect takes the process one step farther, claiming that the gardener's perception of the rope is also false. Why would that be? Because the final illusion is life itself, yet the illusion is quite real in that anything that lives must have an experience of that life, or as Thomas Nagel suggested in his thought experiment, there must be something that it is like for any living creature to be what it is.

In Buddhist ontology the elemental constituents of sentient beings are deemed psycho-physical, somewhat like Aristotle's *hylomorphism*, except more a synthesis of mind and form rather than

THE UNICORN PROBLEM

matter and form. Upon inspection, these elements must also be "wholes containing parts", i.e. it is not possible to refine existence down to some irreducible constituent. Unlike Aristotelian logic, Buddhism allows the infinite regress to run unbridled, wild Unicorn that it is, until it reaches a conceptual impasse (Greek: *aporia*).

This impasse points to the Buddhist notion of emptiness, which is not a thing, but rather a conceptual limit. Therefore the root contemplation in regard to Buddhist ontology is that of impermanence: in Buddhist thought, all things are empty of self-inherent being because there is no independent self, and all composites, including our bodies and its constituents, are transitory. Due to this ephemeral quality of existence, all of Being is deemed illusory – the realm of Samsara (In this light, it is very close to Heraclitus and others in the Western tradition). All of this necessarily hinges on Buddhist epistemology and its ultimate reliance upon personal experience through meditative practices.

Thus Buddhists claim life is dream-like and, like all dreams, afflicted by impermanence and run through and through with hollow forms. Nonetheless, although we may call that dream an illusion, the fact of its occurrence remains undeniable. Nonetheless, it is the nature of human experience itself that is being called into question. In our Western philosophical tradition, Rene Descartes asked himself if he could know for certain that what he called his waking life – the so-called facts of his existence – was naught but an ongoing dream. His answer? No, he could not. He might be experiencing a false awakening. He could be dreaming that he is sitting in an outdoor Café in Paris, sipping espresso and chatting about philosophy or mathematics or Newton's theory of gravity, when in truth he is sleeping soundly in his bed (which, rumor has it, he was fond of doing). His personal experiences could be nothing but illusions, just as we refer to dreams as illusions.

We have dreams...yes. But most of us feel that they are qualitatively different from our waking life. But for Buddhists and Rene Descartes, this is not the case, because what is real in all of our experiences is their absolute impermanence and uncertainty, and thus their illusory nature. I believe Heraclitus would agree, insisting that it is a mistake to assume that anything could "be" or actually exist in the first place. He is not denying phenomena, insisting that nothing actually appears before us. He is instead suggesting that our experiences appear to us as real, but their true nature is ephemeral, and perhaps forever unknowable. As Bertrand Russell remarked:

"…What we directly see and feel is merely 'appearance', which we believe to be a sign of some 'reality' behind. But if the reality is not what appears, have we any means of knowing whether there is any reality at all? And if so, have we any means of finding out what it is like?"

Despite what we discover about our universe, either empirically or purely theoretically, the search for an abiding permanence continues. It is the same search that has occupied humankind for centuries. We know that Heraclitus for one, could not abandon the notion that within this eternal flux, coursing through the very flames of unpredictability, there was order, an internal harmony. This was a narrative similar to that of Pythagoras when he announced that "God is number," and again centuries later when Newton announced that God was a mathematician. Recently a contemporary cosmologist affirmed this same claim and announced that the universe is mathematics, such that in principle we will someday be able to understand the entire Cosmos. All of these profound thinkers concluded that not only is the Cosmos orderly and imbued with Logos (a kind of Divine Reason), but that rational creatures such as we could understand it.

"In the modern world Pythagoras is most of all famous as a mathematician, because of the theorem named after him, and secondarily as a cosmologist, because of the striking view of a universe ascribed to him in the later tradition, in which the heavenly bodies produce 'the music of the spheres' by their movements." – S.E.P.

According to his analysis, Pythagoras demonstrated that music was but the effects of mathematical ratios, numerical expressions that explained the relationship of one tone to another and contained a rational and elegant formula hidden within the sound and the whole of Nature herself.

In the twentieth century, many scientists reclaimed this notion of an internal harmony once again, arguing against those skeptics in the postmodern period of science and philosophy who dogmatically maintained that rational demonstrations were construed, and could not be expected to reveal anything commensurable with an internal harmony or divine order. In the final analysis, this means that reality as we describe it is not an existential fact but more a product of our minds that have been strongly biased by cultural influences. For these postmodern critics of the scientific method, reality is primarily a social construct: human beings possess knowledge strictly in a relative sense, dependent on time, place, and current conditions. All human knowledge is simply the means by which we organize our experiences and not a glimpse into the actual facts of our existence. These are the views of a new breed of Plato's Earth Giants: all truth is *human* truth; all truth is contingent truth (Buddhists would call this relative truth as compared with absolute Truth).

When Plato spoke metaphorically of the war between the Gods and the Earth-Giants, the gods were akin to Plato himself, who posited a type of knowledge that was transcendent of opinions or beliefs. This knowledge was purported to be timeless and universal, knowledge that was the essence of Wisdom itself. As an example of this immutable kind of knowledge, we could speculate that the earth will someday suffer a heat death along with the rest of our solar system. Scientists predict that at some instant about three or four billion years from now, our little insignificant sun will go supernova, and when it does, we go with it. Existence as we know it will return to stardust. Still, if enough time passes—say another six billion or so years – another earth could be formed out of the stellar dust, evolution could run its natural course and humans could arise again, beginning perhaps as bands of curious primates somehow intrigued by their very existence...and the Pythagorean theorem would be as true in this new earth system as it was in the old.

For Plato and succeeding generations of strict rationalists

within philosophy, knowledge in an absolute sense was indeed possible. No equivocations could alter the fact that the shortest distance between two points is a straight line. This was a universal and timeless truth known with absolute certainty, axiomatic until it was shown to be in error. In curved space, such as that in which we live, a parabolic line could be the shortest distance between two points, say, the two cities of London and New York. The airline industry demonstrates this reality every day with the shortest flights possible across the Atlantic. Newton proclaimed that space is uniform (as did Euclid before him), an empty container that in no way influenced the bodies that moved within it, and that time was constant, the clock of the universe always repeating the same tick-tock interval with no variation. Despite the errors of these conclusions, this was taken as Gospel, nigh on to revelatory in nature. According to Newton, God's design was now uncovered and absolute Truth stood naked for the gazing. A Logos permeated the transitive nature of reality, and so for a modern natural philosopher such as Rene' Descartes, the universe was bound together by the intrinsic logic of cause and effect, operating like a gigantic mechanical device, where each gear nestles perfectly into its predetermined niche. For the ancient natural philosopher Heraclitus, the Cosmos was paradoxically both knowable and beyond human conception.

Today's Earth Giants would still argue that all of truth is but truth from a particular vantage point, a judgment that is necessarily the result of being a human being. Thus garbage to mankind is gold to goats. In addition, all knowledge suffers from the throes of historicity. Euclid claimed his axioms were self-evident truths, meaning they required no justification to support their reality – until of course, they were shown to be wrong. Newton had nailed the fundamental structures of the universe to the wall, showing us timeless, eternal truths about the world in which we lived, and then Einstein tore those pictures down. Knowledge that is timeless should by definition be without these historical revisions.

Many other examples of these unjustified "changeless" truths

THE UNICORN PROBLEM

abound. In his time, Aristotle asserted such seemingly self-evident truths as a stationary earth in the center of the Cosmos, a Cosmos that was a finite, closed system. Much later, Copernicus, Galileo, and Kepler demonstrated the flaws in this view of reality. The Catholic Church, which for centuries had embraced Aristotle's view of logic and metaphysics, was far slower than the scientific community in abandoning these obviously outdated versions of knowledge and truth. Most religions are, predictably, resistant to change, as are most large social institutions. Churches have been especially hesitant to embrace the revelations of modern scientific knowledge. They prefer consistency in their truths, and so revealed scriptures necessarily hold preeminence over the empirical claims of science.

***

As we have already discovered, another solution to the same problem of immutability would be to allow that the world is composed of more than one substance. We then might claim the existence of an essence distinct from physical matter, a Separate substance that defies any common physical description—the *psyche, mind, soul, divine witness* or *rigpa*... call it what we might. (As mentioned previously in this text, I prefer the term *pre-conceptual presence*). Regardless, physical matter occupies space; the mind or soul does not. All matter possesses form. The mind or soul has no form, remaining as the epitome of simplicity itself. God also is beyond the pale of physicality. According to the Hellenistic Jewish theologian, Philo (20 B.C.–50 A.D.), God has no name, cannot change, and is absolutely self-sufficient; God simply exists, and our souls are so similar in nature as to be identical with this formless Reality, all of this echoing the ancient Vedic scriptures and the pristine immutability of the *Atman (Brahman)* and its intrinsic relationship with the individual, the *Purusha*.

In like fashion, the pre-Socratic natural philosophers attempted to explain how the world was both simple and permanent (immutable). Their central theme was to show that the complex world had an underpinning to its reality comprised of a single kind of "stuff" from which all else emerges, i.e., a substance, producing attributes and its modes. Their inquiry ignited arguments over the relationship between Being and Becoming, an ontological argument that continues to this day, especially in the various philosophical schools of the East. Today's Western physics, having peered deeply into the properties of physical reality, has pronounced that the universe is composed of matter and energy (although anti-matter and dark energy have recently entered the picture); and that we are, as are all physical things, compounds of mass and energy, what Buddhists would call aggregates. And that which is composed of parts will also, at some point in time, decompose. Our physicality eventually transposes into a condition we call death, the elements that comprise our forms literally falling apart. However, according to philosophers like Socrates and theologians like St. Augustine, the soul does not suffer this ignominious demise; the soul is simple, composed of no parts, hence incapable of coming apart, in a word, immortal...and perhaps, immutable. Rene Descartes would argue against the materialists and empiricists of his time by reprising this ancient view of two substances, claiming that existence is dualistic by nature, one side of *body* and the other of *mind*.

In the Christian doctrine as inherited from the early theologians, all material forms – ourselves included – were deemed contingent, merely temporary phenomena that required a composite of elements in order to exist at all. In Buddhism, this same organizational principle is referred to as *interdependent origination.* According to this view, all phenomena requires outside assistance in order to be at all – material forms are peninsulas, not islands. Nothing, with the sole exception of Buddha Mind (or God in our monotheistic traditions), is beyond this interdependent nature. We look at a tree, and think simply *tree*. But there is no tree per se, but rather the complex aggregate of elements – soil, water, air, and so on – without which the tree could not exist. No thing or person has self-inherent being, hence the notion of the emptiness and the impermanence of all phenomena in Buddhist ontology, epistemology and metaphysics.

In the ontology and metaphysics of Christianity, God replaces Buddha Mind as the only self-sufficient being, depending on nothing else but Himself in order to be (I say Him because the monotheistic traditions we are addressing are all paternalistic in origin). Only God is beyond interdependent origination. Since the universe must have been created by something, God is a necessary being. Buddha Mind shares this same attribute of being necessary or intrinsic to all phenomena, whereas we and all other natural forms are merely *contingent* beings. We could just as easily be here or not.

Hence, to address that which is immutable is to speak of God or Buddha Mind.

In the Buddhist descriptions of Pure Awareness (*Rig-pa*) the similarities with the ancient Greek definition of the psyche are striking. The soul (psyche) and the Tibetan Buddhist conception of pure awareness are both deemed the ground or seat of our thoughts, feelings, and perceptions (i.e., the *Knower*). So in this sense, the situation is necessarily very personal; my experiences or your experiences are all we have to go on. Within this contingent and biased outlook however, lies the Truth-Body that supersedes the physical body – although not completely distinct from physical form, and therefore not dependent on physical matter for its existence—a substrate of sorts.

Pure Awareness is also directly associated with the great expanse of the Dharmakaya, just as the air within a cup participates fully in the atmosphere above it; our mind, soul, or rig-pa connects in some mysterious manner to our physical form, but nonetheless remains essentially formless. Paradoxically Buddhists add to these descriptions by claiming that in Buddhist ontology, there is no soul. When the Buddha was asked if a true self exists or whether we possess a soul, he refused to answer (It is said that his silence was thunderous). Add to this the doctrine of the Buddhist dialectician Nagarjuna, wherein he states that existence neither is nor is not, and we are ultimately left to conclude that no final truth about our souls or our physical existence is possible.

The idea of emptiness (*shunyata*) in Buddhism — numerically translated as zero — takes on an entirely different significance, in that emptiness is definitely not "nothing." Many of us would then ask: If not nothing...then what? And according to Nagarjuna, the dualistic conceptual process gallops away on yet another Unicorn. Is it true, as the major religions both East and West believe, that we live in a moral universe? Who knows the truthful answer to that question? Is there a need for a path of virtue and a code of conduct for the human realm? The answer to that is one that each of us must decide both privately and collectively as a society, and I would say is a no-brainer.

Some of the teachings in the religious and philosophical schools of India are nearly synonymous with the traditional attributes we assign to our monotheistic God of the West. In the Vedic explanation, for example, the individual soul (the *Purasha*, or in some instances, the *Atman*) is but the parking space of Brahman, the Universal Soul or Spirit. The dominant attributes of this Universal Soul include omniscience, omnipotence, omnipresence and so on. In addition to being described as both simple and immortal, Brahman is also claimed to be the ground or seat of all phenomenal existence, including the essence of human nature—our true Self. Translating this into Vajrayana Buddhist terms, we might say that the essence of all sentient beings is one and the same as the Dharmakaya, that realm of radiant Pure Mind (Grk. *Nous*)—once again, the Truth Body.

In our Western philosophical traditions, we find that Bishop Berkeley also proposed a variation of this Mind-Only view of reality, initiating what philosophers categorize as *Idealism*. For both Buddhists and to a degree, Berkeley, there is but one substance: Mind. Buddhists call this the Mind of Buddha — our essential or awakened nature – whereas the good Bishop spoke of the one Mind as the Mind of God.

In all of the above descriptions, we find at least one constant abiding through each of the narratives: immutability. For the ancient Greeks such as Socrates, the soul may continuously move, separating

THE UNICORN PROBLEM

from our bodies once we die. But its fundamental attribute is timelessness itself: The soul never dies. Its nature is constant and unchanging, which is how simple things necessarily must be. For Buddhists, the realm of Pure Awareness shares this same attribute of eternal constancy, a truth always present within us, even when we remain ignorant of this pre-conceptual reality…as we somnambulists are wont to do. Buddha Mind requires no object to discern, no thought to pay attention to, and no sentiment to feel in order to be what it is, despite the fact that it is the prevailing ground or essence of all these activities. The psyche or soul, it seems, likewise inhabits these activities, yet remains simultaneously distinct from them.

Whether we call it the soul or Pure Awareness, this distinct characteristic of immutability—something so simple it cannot be altered – is what separates it from the ordinary realm of physical stuff. As discussed previously, all physical stuff is constantly on the move, doing its best to approach the speed of light, or contrarily, to slow into the illusion of stillness. Phenomena are ultimately unreachable in any conceptual manner due to their constantly shifting manifestations, and as Kant advised, we may never know the "thing-in-itself". If experience is what we feel, think, and speak about, the essential problem lies in the relationship between our individual experiences – which are necessarily contingent and particular – and Reality with a capital R. The immediate condition appears to be that our experiences are unique and constantly shifting, whereas we would hope that Reality—if it exists at all – is at least constant; it should remain the same no matter who's peering into it.

In science, it is physics that explains, predicts, and ultimately controls the objects that move in space and time—human beings included. Therefore scientists need to be ready to change their understanding—their hypotheses and theories – if the observations and data require it. Yet the principles that animate phenomena are (hopefully) unchanging, or even if they are indeed changing, we can still ask: what is the pattern of that change? Which algorithm will enable us to predict the next move within this flux?

What are the laws—the constants – of physics? Aren't they our most generalized description of bodies in motion and their perpetually shifting relationships? And what does this description look like? Frankly, the pictures aren't pretty: they're discombobulating. And the math? The quintessence of complication! After all, what does a force *look* like? Prior and up to the modern period of the natural sciences (15th to 19th centuries), for most of the natural philosophers (scientists) mathematics was not essential for a true understanding of nature. A pictorial representation was sufficient. Today, like the view of Pythagoras some two-thousand years ago, the modern scientist understands that nature can best be understood via mathematics: the scientific description of phenomena is functionally oriented, and the descriptions of those processes are steeped in highly abstract mathematical formulations that attempt to make sense of the empirical evidence. It's worth noting that inscribed over the entrance to Plato's Academy – our first Western Educational Institute – were the words, "Let No One Ignorant of Geometry Enter."

The quest for Truth, I would submit, has always been the search for the immutable. When natural philosophers began reading the book of nature earnestly, studying the bits of information written therein and then generalizing certain laws that organized all of that information, they desired knowledge that was timeless, universal, necessary, and certain. They were not in search of principles that were valid today but void tomorrow or that proved to be little more than distorted versions of reality produced by the human mind. Reality was presumed to be independent of that particular organ. And as a consequence, if universal and timeless truths are captured, one can begin speaking seriously about the nature of Reality (or at least, so goes the thinking).

Even logic, that primary means by which we are supposed to know with certainty if a given proposition is either true or false, rests upon fundamental principles known as laws. Without assuming these laws to be self-evident – the perpetual operators behind the scene – then nothing can be known beyond all doubt; these laws are the rules of the reasoning game, at least as far as pure logic is concerned. If these principles don't hold as necessarily true, then it's hard to

THE UNICORN PROBLEM

imagine how human knowledge could ever move beyond opinions and beliefs. Our conceptual artifacts would always fail us. When we speak of certainty – *that about which we could not possibly be wrong* – we are, if nothing else, sensing a taste of the immutable.

How would we describe this Mysterious Immutable? Isn't it assumed as always present? How could it not be? Early Church theologians spoke of *"the mystery that attracts* (Lat. *mysterim fascinosum*)

"...by which humans are irresistibly drawn to the glory, beauty, adorable quality, and the blessing, redeeming, and salvation-bringing power of transcendence. All of these features are present in the Christian concepts of God...."

***

When you and I are in the same room, don't we implicitly agree that we are having a real experience as opposed to, say, a dream experience...that Reality is present for both of us? And yet if someone were to ask us to describe our personal experiences of that reality, those personal experiences might be much different. I think the room is too cold, you think the temperature is just right. I think the chairs we are sitting in are too hard, and you think they are perfectly fine. I call the color of the cup purple; you say it looks more like indigo. Like the story of Goldilocks and the Three Bears, each of us is seeking a comfortable fit within this common reality that we apparently share. (In Buddhist and Hindu philosophy, the word *dukkha*, or what is usually translated as suffering, literally means "misfit"). So if our experiences are so different from one another, what is it that isn't different for each of us? Reality must be the answer to that question, but it seems that pinning down this common denominator is not as simple as we make it sound.

If I taste a particular kind of ice cream, say mocha java (one of my favorites) and you find vanilla much more to your liking, we don't argue over who's right or wrong about this; we agree that we all have different tastes. But if I say it's cold outside and you say it's not, who's right? Is there a "right" in this situation? We could of course resort to a temperature gauge and specify the exact temperature in numbers, but that wouldn't actually answer the question for us. What it would do is establish a norm, a temperature—say 72 degrees—that we might agree is pleasant for most male human beings who weigh around one-hundred fifty-five pounds. Beyond that, how do we know that the reading of 72 degrees is correct? Use another gauge to double check? But what if that one is inaccurate as well? How would we know with certainty that the number given and the actual temperature are the same? And if the gauge reading is 72, and I say it's chilly and you say it's too warm, aren't we both right and wrong at the same time? If it is cold to me and hot to you, then that's the simple truth of our experience. Does an objective measure of air temperature fall under the same rubric as personal taste? That doesn't sound right. In addition, if the atmosphere is made up of gasses and those gasses are themselves comprised of atoms, is there such a thing as hot and cold atoms? That doesn't seem right either.

As one of the originators of the atomistic theory Democritus argued: "By convention sweet and by convention bitter, by convention hot, by convention cold, by convention color; in reality atoms and void."

But the atomistic explanation has its own problems. Even Democritus and Leucippus realized that when the atoms irritated our sense fields and thereby generated our perceptions, these perceptions were necessarily one or two steps removed from the actual object perceived. The epistemological concern was that the world as we perceive it might actually be a mistaken view, and that somehow our minds might overturn Reality itself.

"Democritus apparently recognized that his view gives rise to an epistemological problem: it takes our knowledge of the world to be derived from our sense experience, but the senses themselves not to be in direct contact with the nature of things, thus leaving room for omission or error." – *S.E.P.*

In order to clarify this problem of what constitutes the Reality of our experience versus our personal bias and filtering of what appears to us, the philosopher John Locke proposed two categories or qualities of perception, one primary and the other secondary. Already accepting the laws, axioms and postulates of Newton's corpuscular physics (and by implication those of Democritus), Locke granted an inherent power to matter itself. He admitted that in actuality we don't perceive matter, which is quite a concession from an ardent empiricist who insisted that all knowledge comes to us from the sense fields alone. He also claimed that at birth human sentiency is but a blank tablet (tabla rasa) to be written upon by the world that awaits it.

But even if matter, which functions as the substance or glue that holds all appearances together, never reveals itself directly to our sense fields and so must remain a conceptual inference, according to Locke this material stuff generates our perceptions, cognitions, remembrances, and so on; it possesses that kind of power. Hence there are primary sensations we receive directly from an independent, objective world, and so we can rest assured that they are Real in the most simple sense of that word: they are to be understood as the immediate report of how the world truly is. At this level, what we perceive and what is Real correspond perfectly.

"The Primary qualities of an object are those whose existence is independent of the existence of a perceiver. Locke's inventory of primary qualities included shape, size, position, number, motion-or-rest and solidity, and science claims to be completing this inventory by positing such properties as charge, spin and mass."

Secondary qualities however, are different. Although they also originate from the underlying power of matter, they are particular and not universal by nature, altered within our sense fields by the mere facts of our being sentient and human. So even though atoms may not contain a single degree of heat within them, they can certainly produce the effect of very painful surface when I inadvertently lean up against a blazing woodstove. The atoms producing this heat may be excited, but they are decidedly not "hot." Yet to me the heat of the stove is very real. Heat then is a secondary quality of perception, inherent to the human condition but not to Reality itself. Secondary qualities generate a representation of reality, and in that sense they remain one step removed from the immediacy of existence. This view is termed indirect realism or representative realism.

As Locke explains: "The secondary qualities of objects, however, are those properties that do depend on the existence of a perceiver. They can either be seen as properties that are not actually possessed by the objects themselves, or, as dispositional properties, properties that objects only have when considered in relation to their perceivers."

Although dependent upon the direct transmission from a timeless and universal Reality, the human response to that Reality is to various degrees conditioned and thereby transformed. In today's parlance, we might label this form of alteration as a "transduction." Thus the secondary qualities also include color, smell, taste, and texture.

As Locke says: "Such qualities which in truth are nothing in the objects themselves, but powers to produce various sensations in us by their primary qualities."

Returning to a more ancient view, Plato offers us a radically different approach to defining Reality, minus the limitations of human bias. In his view, all perceptions are a form of illusion, and he refutes the notion that the opinions and beliefs that result from our sense fields can be trusted in any complete manner. Perceptual reports are inherently flawed because they seek truth and knowledge in a realm filled with deceptive images. He refers to this habitat as The Cave. For Plato, Reality and Truth are transcendent, a realm of Pure Ideas forever abiding above and beyond the limitations of time and space.

THE UNICORN PROBLEM

	METAPHYSICS	EPISTEMOLOGY	
INTELLIGIBLE	Higher Forms	Understanding	**KNOWLEDGE**
	Mathematical Forms	Reason	
VISIBLE	Sensible Particulars	Perception	**OPINION**
	Images	Imagination	

In an attempt to illustrate further what he means by knowledge and wisdom, Plato offers his Divided Line: To Plato most of us function at the level of conjecture and belief (doxa), which is not to say that opinions and beliefs serve no function. When I take an umbrella with me before I leave the house, I am acting on the belief that it will rain, and this belief will serve me well if in fact it does rain (in the words of pragmatists such as William James, it pays off). When I stick the key in the ignition of my car, I believe the car will start. This is a helpful belief, or I might walk about town all day, convinced that there was no point in carrying car keys at all. Sometimes of course, this belief does not pay off and the car refuses to start. Out of gas, perhaps? Or dead battery? Now deductive logic kicks in, determining that the engine failure is due somehow to either a lack of fuel, fire, or air, each a necessary condition, and collectively the sufficient conditions for satisfactory motoring.

But if it is Truth and Knowledge we are seeking, then it is important to peer beyond the flux of phenomena in order to understand the principles that actually produce the show. This is the realm of 'episteme' for Plato, examples of which include mathematics and geometry. For the most part, contemporary science and especially mathematics, serve as the primary instantiations of this kind of knowledge. Notwithstanding the fundamental discrepancy between pure theory and applied science, this is where the central laws and principles of nature are revealed and where the presumed causes for the effects we experience serve as explanations for all phenomena. Again, in Aristotle's words: "Happy is the person who knows the cause of things."

The final stage of Plato's divided line is the realm of Sophia. Here we become aware of his Pure Forms. And contrary to the logical demonstrations required for scientific knowledge, even for Plato's own episteme, this knowledge is necessarily intuitive. At this elevated level, Sophia is the illumination of the inherent unity and simplicity of Truth, Beauty, Knowledge, and Justice – collectively, the essential qualities of the ultimate Good, later referred to as the One by the Neo-Platonists. The assumption underlying this notion of the Pure Forms is that the Universe possesses an internal harmony or order *(Logos)* that is ultimately knowable, even by such simpleminded creatures as we. If this is true, what a gift the Universe has bestowed upon humanity: we all become the Universe gazing upon itself.

***

Buddhists maintain that human minds are filled with various mixtures of illusion, confusion and self-delusion, misguided opinions and beliefs about reality and truth that are off track. The true destination and final guide – Reality – lies deep within, where the central characteristic of the human mind, in Buddhist metaphor, is the wish-fulfilling jewel. But since most (if not all) of us use our minds to calculate our next move in nature's system of survival, it's not likely that we would ordinarily describe or perceive our own mind's primary quality as being such a gem. According to Buddhist doctrine however, it is possible to realize and make effective use of this true nature of the mind and thus live a fully actualized life. The good news is that we are all potentially Buddhas; every human mind harbors this jewel within.

Much like the hero in Plato's Allegory of the Cave, each and every person, regardless of circumstance, is deemed capable of overcoming the darkness created by his or her inaccurate perceptions and beliefs and can awaken to the Reality revealed by the full light of day. And wouldn't we have to admit that Plato's ultimate Good – symbolized by the Sun as the orb of illumination – is at least analogous to the Buddhist notion of Ultimate Reality? Some Buddhist doctrines claim that the essence of the human mind, once apprehended clearly, is pure light. Once again we see that philosophy, like religion, is similarly concerned with awakening to final Truths beyond mere *doxa*, beyond our mundane, habitual opinions and beliefs that guide nearly every thought and action in our normal daily lives.

Though this quality of consistent awareness is the similarly desired goal for those on the Buddhist path, it is achieved through different stages. For instance, in the early development of Buddhism, living a virtuous or moral life was the primary antidote to personal suffering; i.e., moral conduct would slowly lead the adept away from categorical ignorance and into liberation from rebirth. Although the moral admonitions remains important, Buddhists of the Tibetan Vajrayana system go about matters a bit differently and practice (as mentioned earlier), what is called Generation Stage.

In Generation Stage the practitioner visualizes him or herself (and all others) as a member of one of the five deity families. The particular deity of Generation Stage practice is associated with the personality type of the practitioner – a categorization of personality types which, we should note, has a long history within our own Western culture and correlates very well with our various psychological traditions and systems. On a practical level, Generation Stage practice is intended to remove obstacles within our personalities, turning the "poisons into medicine," i.e. transforming personal suffering into personal bliss (I'm still on the wait-list). If we were to wonder how any of this could ever produce the impressive effects promised, we are reminded that it is because we all possess the potential for Buddha Nature. My ordinary mind may feel like a torture devise of my own design, but in actuality the intrinsic essence of my mind and the mind of everyone else is said to be Buddha Mind, that precious jewel that awaits actualization within us. Simply getting a quick sense of this ontological and metaphysical essence is sufficient to impart a degree of wisdom to the fortunate practitioner. Thus the deity represents this essential nature we all share.

Although Plato did not advise visualization practices, or at least none that we know of beyond Socrates' *daimon,* and though his metaphors may be different from those in Buddhist doctrines, the motivation and goal is consistent between both Platonic philosophy and Buddhist practice: seek wisdom and find the Truth. The goal for both is to realize the immutable nature of all phenomena. The underlying assumption is that Truth does not change. For Plato this was the geometric realm of Pure Forms and the unassailable nature of the Good, and in Buddhist thought this Truth resides solely in direct cognition and the awakening of the pre-conceptual presence within all sentient beings. The entrance signpost to these insights should read: "No Unicorns Allowed."

CHAPTER 9
EMBRACING DOUBT

"Doubt is the essence of faith"
Owen Meany (John Irving)

THE SIMULATION ARGUMENT

"Many works of science fiction as well as some forecast by serious technologists and futurologists predict that enormous amounts of computing power will be available in the future. Let us suppose for a moment that these predictions are correct. One thing that later generations might do with their super-powerful computers is run detailed simulations of their forebears or of people like their forebears. Because their computer would be so powerful, they could run a great many such simulations. Suppose that these simulated people are conscious (as they would be if the simulations were sufficiently fine-grained and if a certain quite widely accepted position in the philosophy of mind is correct). Then it could be the case that the vast majority of minds like ours do not belong to the original race but rather to people simulated by the advanced descendants of an original race. It is then possible to argue that, if this were the case, we would be rational to think that we are likely among the simulated minds rather than among the original biological ones. Therefore, if we don't think that we are currently living in a computer simulation, we are not entitled to believe that we will have descendants who will run lots of such simulations of their forebears." – *Dr. Nick Bostrom, Oxford University Philosophy*

THE UNICORN PROBLEM

LIVING WITHOUT UNICORNS

At this point we might be wondering if we can ever distinguish between what we believe is the truth as opposed to what is actually the truth. It may be that Bertrand Russell is correct when he counsels that we must learn to live with the uncertainty that underlies all human knowledge, while at the same time exhorting us to move beyond the profound doubt that pierces the heart of human sentience. He also advises that, from the philosophical view, our realization that a question is unanswerable is "as complete an answer as any that could possibly be obtained." Is he correct, or should we instead embrace the intriguing position of Ludwig Wittgenstein, who maintained that doubt arises only when a solution is known to be possible?

One response to these concerns comes from C. Bobonich, a classical – Greek scholar from the Stanford philosophy department. He recently gave a series of lectures at our university, and I was fortunate enough to have him lead one of my classes, where he "riffed" (his own term) on ancient Greek philosophy for about an hour. Towards the end of his talk, one of the students asked him where he stood in regard to the various philosophical issues raised, especially the issue of certain knowledge. He responded by saying he was one of the few in his department who would call himself a "skeptic." Despite having been raised as a Catholic, he claimed to be an epistemic agnostic, since he had serious doubts when he was asked to accept final conclusions regarding absolute Truth. He then recounted to the class the tale of the ancient Greek philosopher Pyrrho (360-270 BCE), the inspirational leader of the first Greek school of radical skepticism.

Although there are differing accounts as to how radical Pyrrho was in his skepticism, one is as follows: "...Diogenes (9.62) reports Antigonus as saying that Pyrrho's lack of trust in his senses led him to ignore precipices, oncoming wagons and dangerous dogs, and that his friends had to follow him around to protect him from these various everyday hazards." – *S.E.P.*

MITCHELL J. FRANGADAKIS

Broadly speaking, there are two differing types of skepticism: philosophical skepticism such as that of Pyrrho, and ordinary incredulity. The original definition and character of a philosophical skeptic is that of a seeker, or "one who inquires." By its nature, this perpetuates or affirms a process of doubting: philosophical skeptics would simultaneously doubt both the absolute Truth (as proclaimed by Plato's Gods and other Dogmatists), as well as the relativists' view of the Earth Giants and our postmodern deconstructionists, wherein even the foundational premises of scientific validation are deemed imputations of Truth. However, being a skeptic of this sort does not entail the automatic rejection of common sense or beliefs regarding moral conduct. Global skeptics reject extreme views in general but do not reject the practice of honest inquiry.

As for ordinary skepticism, the doubts that dart around us on any ordinary day, the Stanford Encyclopedia of Philosophy offers the following example:

"Suppose Anne believes that the bird she is looking at is a robin and I believe that if she were to look carefully, she would see that its coloration is not quite that of a robin…and that it flies somewhat differently than robins do. Thus, there are two grounds for doubting that Anne knows that it is a robin:

a. The color of this bird isn't typical of robins.
b. The flight pattern of this bird is not typical of robins.

This is a case of ordinary doubt because there are, in principle, two general ways that are available for removing the grounds for doubt:

a. The alleged grounds for doubt could be shown to be false;
b. Or, it could be shown that grounds for doubt, though true, can be neutralized."

THE UNICORN PROBLEM

In the same article it is pointed out that Anne could be shown the Audubon Field Guide for Birds, where there are many pictures of robins with the same coloration. As a consequence, the first ground for doubt is shown to be false. And the other cause for doubt regarding the bird's flight pattern could be neutralized if upon closer inspection it is found that some of the robin's tail feathers are missing, causing its erratic flight. Thus we have explained away, or at least neutralized, both grounds for doubt.

Again, in all ordinary instances of incredulity, the doubt in principle can be removed.

Philosophical or global skepticism in its most ardent form argues that there is no way, even in principle, to remove all doubt from truth-bearing claims. This is not the dour attitude of a lifelong pessimist, but simply an attempt to acknowledge the given facts of our situation. After all, many contemporary critics might justifiably claim that philosophy has been rehearsing the same questions for over 2500 years, and still the curtain has not dropped and no final scripts are forthcoming. It is as though we are actors trapped in a Platonic Matrix, conjuring justifications for our cherished convictions while at the same time engaged in chasing shadows on the wall.

As Chenjeri states: "Much of epistemology has arisen either in defense of or in opposition to various forms of skepticism. Indeed, one could classify various theories of knowledge by their responses to skepticism. For example, rationalists could be viewed as skeptical about the possibility of empirical knowledge while not being skeptical with regard to a priori knowledge and empiricists could be seen as skeptical about the possibility of a priori knowledge but not so with regard to empirical."

In his *Meditations*, Descartes held to a global form of skepticism in that he doubted all phenomena, including his own reasoned judgments: "If you would be a real seeker after truth", he said, "it is necessary that at least once in your life you doubt, as far as possible, all things." Ultimately however, he concluded that he could not doubt that there must a doubter who doubts – a thinker who is thinking. This was a judgment he believed to be clear and distinct and, therefore, irrefutable – in effect, a self-evident truth. Thus contemporary rationalists might contend that Descartes overcame the impasse created by skepticism since doubt in and of itself was the firm foundation for the assembly of Truth. Skeptics, on the other hand, would deny Descartes his refuge in this self-evident truth, this foundational premise which claims that if he thinks, then there must be a thinker: *cogito ergo sum*. From this view, all he actually demonstrated as certain is that experiences occur. Their exact nature, including whether or not there is truly a subject for these experiences, or Descartes' "thinking thing," remains dubitable as opposed to self-evident. Nonetheless, what philosophical skeptics seriously question is whether any foundational system of justification for beliefs is even possible.

"… Philosophical skepticism about a proposition of a certain type derives from considerations that are such that they cannot be removed by appealing to additional propositions of that type…" – *S.E.P.*

In 1981, the philosopher Hilary Putnam (1926-2016) formulated the intriguing Brain-in-a-Vat thought experiment, in which he asked if it was possible to know with complete confidence that we aren't simply neurons floating in a bath of sustaining chemicals, all of our experiences being nothing more than simulated programs plugged into and run by a vast computer. He asks us to imagine that all of this is taking place sometime in the distant future, but the program informs us that we are actually living in the current time — which (since we have been told this experience takes place in the distant future) is already past. This rings the same kind of bell as does Bertrand Russell's question: How do we know that the universe didn't start 10 seconds—or 10 minutes or 10 days – ago?

"If I accept the argument, I must conclude that a brain in a vat can't think truly that it is a brain in a vat, even though others can think this about it. What follows? Only that I cannot express my skepticism by saying 'Perhaps I am a brain in a vat.' Instead I must

THE UNICORN PROBLEM

say 'Perhaps I can't even think the truth about what I am, because I lack the necessary concepts and my circumstances make it impossible for me to acquire them'. If this doesn't qualify as skepticism, I don't know what does!" – *T.Nagel*

A contemporary variation of Descartes's Evil Genius argument of the 1700's is Dr. Bostrom's Simulation Argument cited at the beginning of this chapter. We might easily trace a direct line from these thought experiments back to Plato's Allegory of the Cave. However, the more contemporary versions are illustrations of a more radical skepticism then even Plato was willing to accept. They ask, "How do you know that it is not the case that…(fill in the blank)?" which is to ask exactly how we are able to demonstrate beyond all doubt that the conclusion – be it the work of an evil genius or some self-conscious computer in the future – is falsifiable? The syllogistic form of this type of argument goes as follows:

"Let P stand for any belief or claim about the external world, such as fire is hot or snow is white.
    P1. If I know that P, then I know that I am not a brain in a vat.
    P 2. I do not know that I am not a brain in a vat
    Thus, I do not know that P.

"Putnam thus stipulates that *all* sentient beings are brains in a vat, hooked up to one another through a powerful computer that has no programmer: 'that's just how the universe is'. We are then asked, given at least the *physical* possibility of this scenario, whether we could say or think it. Putnam answers that we could not: the assertion "we are brains in a vat" would be sense self-refuting in the same way that the general statement 'all general statements are false' is." – *I.E.P.*

We could conclude that any argument that offers evidence to substantiate its claim is necessarily a type of self-referencing argument – not a paradox per se – yet beset by its own intrinsic Unicorn nature.

MITCHELL J. FRANGADAKIS

"…The radical hypothesis that we're unjustified in trusting the deliverances of our own reason has the curious quality of simultaneously undermining any response raised against it, on the basis that the reasoning underpinning that very response might itself be faulty…" – *T. Wardman*

***

There is more than a bit of irony in the fact that contemporary science evolved from the intellectual remonstrations of the ancient Skeptics. Science remains part of a philosophical lineage willing to consider that all accepted truths, including even the self-evident truths of common sense, might in fact be false. This attitude advanced a probabilistic rather than absolutists' view of truth (and perhaps Bertrand Russell was spot on when he said that our current notion of common sense is the "metaphysics of the stone age"). Instead of propagating the search for timeless, universal and certain Truths, science now argues over how to best explain, predict, and control nature. Science does not necessarily ask the Why of something, as might Socrates or Aristotle, or for that matter, an alert five-year old child. Science prefers to understand the How of things. For science, truth is how things work.

Nonetheless, the logical positivists, when insisting that all matters of fact and all conditions of truth must fall within the purview of time and space, cannot justify their own criteria for knowledge. If they were to do so, they would violate their own principles, i.e. which events within time and space verify the principle that all knowable facts and truth-bearing claims must fall within time and space? Speaking as strict empiricists, as the logical positivists' rules demand, we find that no such condition is conceivable.

Those of us who agree with Bobonich's epistemological agnosticism most often find ourselves taking the position of *not* taking a position, a none-of-the-above attitude that carries its own moral risks. This is not however a complete refutation of the ordinary facts of experience. Aside from Pyhrro, global skeptics don't dance on the edge of cliffs or step into fires because they believe that sense impressions such as heat cannot be trusted as real. The proverbial school of hard knocks will readily overcome any doubts someone may entertain about gravity, fire and the other pragmatic affairs of mundane existence.

"Skepticism begins when we include ourselves in the world about which we claim knowledge. We notice that certain types of evidence convince us, that we are content to allow justifications of belief come to an end at a certain point, that we feel that we know many things even without knowing or having grounds for believing the denial of others, which, if true, would make what we claim to know false." – *T. Nagel*

The real hazard, as Hume pointed out centuries ago, is that pure reason cannot even assure us that the sun will appear on the Eastern horizon tomorrow – and yet we believe it will. Empirical evidence that claims to assure us of a certain future based on past experiences may generate self-confidence and personal convictions about what is true or not, but leaves irrefutable knowledge out of the picture. Our assurances about the next moment in time arise from the depths of our past experiences, and in that regard, there is no guarantee our predictions about what the future holds are accurate or even truly predictable. Any claims to the contrary have necessarily stepped into the realm of opinion, belief or faith, and faith by definition supersedes all rational considerations. Beliefs express our convictions about what is worthwhile, whereas faith oftentimes serves as the expression of our certitude regarding those principles that we regard as beyond all doubt, no matter what the evidence may evince. Since all of us must feel, think and act in order to live the simplest of lives, we must also continuously construe judgments about truth and reality. But we can never be certain of our understanding of truth and what we deem reality to be.

Even after centuries of research, science offers us no solution to the ambiguity and uncertainty that permeates human existence. In this respect, science and philosophy share similar results in their respective epistemological endeavors. Today we have numerous scientific and quasi-scientific views as to what constitutes ultimate reality, each compelling in its own fashion.

In his book *The Goldilocks Enigma,* the cosmologist Paul Davies offers the following currently prevailing views of metaphysical reality:

> 1) The absurd universe: Our universe just happens to be the way it is; it contains no inherent meaning.
>
> 2) The unique universe: There is a deep underlying unity in physics, which necessitates the universe being the way it is. A scientific "theory of everything" will explain why the various features of the universe must have exactly the values that we see.
>
> 3) The multiverse: Multiple universes exist, having all possible combinations of characteristics, and we inevitably find ourselves within a universe that allows us to exist.
>
> 4) Intelligent Design: A creator designed the universe with the purpose of supporting complexity and the emergence of intelligence.
>
> 5) The life principle: There is an underlying principle that constrains the universe to evolve towards life and mind.
>
> 6) The self-explaining universe: A closed explanatory or causal loop: "perhaps only universes with a capacity for consciousness can exist." This is Wheeler's Participatory Anthropic Principle (PAP).
>
> 7) The fake universe: We live inside a virtual reality, a simulated existence.

Number seven above is the simulated universe proposed by

THE UNICORN PROBLEM

Bostrom's thought experiment, which is a contemporary version of Putnam's Brain-in-a Vat thought experiment and Rene Descartes's Evil Demon Argument. An evil demon or genius, Descartes suggested, could be deceiving me about everything, including simple facts like "fire is hot." In a simulated universe such as described by Bostrom, all facts are fake or illusions, in the sense that they do not necessarily correspond to any actual experiences or reality outside of us. Thus, if we indeed live in a simulated universe, then our reality could be radically altered at any one moment and none of us would be the wiser. Each of us is left to judge for ourselves which version of ultimate reality sounds most plausible, assuming we are concerned about metaphysical speculations at all.

Philosophical inquiry, too, ultimately leaves us on our own. According to Plato, knowledge is but a belief that is both true and demonstrated as such. But we must ask: What kind of demonstration is actually required, and how many times must it be repeated for a claim to be accepted as Truth? And what criteria, including the necessary assumptions that lie under them, should we use as our litmus test? Is simple logic sufficiently stringent if our search requires that the truth we discover be beyond all doubt? On this matter, perhaps we should take counsel from Plato's teacher Socrates, and realize that the heart of wisdom lies in knowing that we don't know and in learning to accept this as a given of human existence. It's possible that he was also making a rhetorical point, thereby illustrating our inability to sufficiently define the very concepts we generate to comprehend reality. Was he suggesting that, perhaps sometime in the future, the answers to his What is it? questions will be answered, and we will know for certain what Truth, Beauty, Justice, and Knowledge are? Or is he chiding us, filling us in on his little secret, showing us the futility of our quest for any final Truth?

"Thus the most radical skeptic may be consoled, without being rebuked or refuted; he may leap at one bound over the whole human tangle of beliefs and dogmatic claims, elude human incapacity and bias, and take hold of the quite sufficient assurance that any essence or ideal quality of being which he may be intuiting has just the characters he is finding in it, and has them eternally." – G. *Santayana*

***

The power of reason can also be explained as an intrinsically adaptive force, and the process of adaptation requires the same kind of creative unpredictability that animated the fire of Heraclitus, the spontaneous and magical display of all phenomena in Buddhism and yes, as Kant might advise, the personal burden of moral duty. Reason condemns us to be creative because it expresses our potential as inherently adaptive animals while exposing the extent of our responsibility for the choices we freely make. It is this very freedom that shapes us into the moral creatures that we are – whether we consciously choose to be so or not. The lion in the jungle by its nature can commit no wrong nor transgress any moral laws. On the other hand, we humans cannot evade our values, judgments and determinations of what we deem to be true and what for us is good —even if all of these prove to be but ineffective attempts at ameliorating our meager mental and emotional capabilities. And though Marcus Aurelius may have been right when he claimed that our lives are but opinions, those opinions greatly influence the very quality of our existence and directly affect the lives of those around us. Another way to make the same point is to suggest that reason is yet another expression of the human will, and the human will is but a particular species of that creative and mysterious current we call Life. Reason doesn't objectively report on existence. Rather, reason is an active participant in existence.

Even if pure reason cannot provide us with brute facts about which we can be certain, this is not to say that no truths can be uncovered. As both Aristotle and Kant reminded, there is a practical form of reason, an exercise of our rational faculty that informs us where to hunt for our next meal, when the stove is too hot to touch, or when to cross the road safely. This flexible and adaptive form of reason, *(phronesis),* is what St. Aquinas referred to as prudence and Aristotle as practical wisdom.

Aristotle described *phronesis* in this way: "...Wisdom to take counsel, to judge the goods and evils and all the things in life that are desirable and to be avoided, to use all the available goods finely, to behave rightly in society, to observe due occasions, to employ both speech and action with sagacity, to have expert knowledge of all things that are useful."

Buddhist ontology supports this view indirectly, claiming that human consciousness is analogous to our other sense fields; consciousness (and reason in particular) is but another faculty by which we glean information from our environment. It's an inquiry into our surroundings that progresses in a natural order from the normal five sense fields but finally culminates in our capacity to think. Through the arrangement of our concepts and the pictorial power of our imagination and memories, we then sort out all of these sense impressions into some organized whole, an index of categories transformed from the flux of existence into relatively static images and fixed rules, or as Bergson suggested, maps of the territory. Consciousness offers us yet another arena of information by which to comprehend who we are, where we are, and perhaps even why we are. Considered this way, consciousness is our sixth sense.

And yet – at the risk of contradicting my previous claims regarding knowledge and certitude – I am obliged to further explain my stance on faith: I have faith in a timeless, universal and certain Truth, with a capital T, that I trust remains available to all of us. And this is a Truth that cannot be determined through reason alone. It rests ultimately on our own informed insight and realization.

Even that radical skeptic Pyrho, the same individual who would walk through campfires because he did not believe that fire was hot, even this radical skeptic had to admit that: "...The nature of the divine and the good is eternal, from which a most even-tempered life for a man is derived." – *S.E.P.*

My faith then may be radically different from what you

understand by that word. Therefore it is important to remember that there are various meanings that each of us attaches to this idea. As mentioned previously, the type of faith I am referring to could be aptly described as purely affective or as an existential confidence. My view of faith – excluding any references to God as an ontological reality – aligns with the description of faith in the Sufi tradition, an essentially mystical path.

"…Faith is thus understood as a kind of knowledge attended by a certainty that *excludes doubt*. But faith will not be exclusively cognitive, if, as in Calvin's definition, of faith – knowledge is not only 'revealed to our minds' but also 'sealed upon our hearts'. For, on this model faith will also have an affective component that includes a welcoming of the knowledge received." – S.E.P.

My understanding could be approached in this way: If one were to strip away all assumptions, opinions, concepts and propositions, what, if anything, would be left? And to this I would answer: faith. Thus my view of faith is also in keeping with the mysticism of the Taoist Chuang Tzu (369-286 BCE).

In offering his comments on this venerable Chinese sage, Thomas Merton observes: "The way of Tao is to begin with the simple good with which one is endowed by the very fact of existence. Instead of self-conscious cultivation of this good (which vanishes when we look at it and becomes intangible when we try to grasp it) we grow quietly in the humility of a simple, life, and this way is analogous (at least psychologically) to the Christian "life of faith."

An ardent Rationalist, of course, might object to these particular sentiments. It appears that faith of this sort attempts to substantiate itself by appealing to mystic revelation, a purely subjective experience as opposed to an objective, empirically justified form of knowledge. Bertrand Russell offers the following observation: "Mysticism is, in essence, little more than a certain intensity and depth of feeling in regard to what is believed about the universe."

Most generally in Buddhist doctrine, faith is the process of *Establishing the View*, and this View begins with the simple act of

THE UNICORN PROBLEM

taking refuge. One takes refuge in the Three Jewels: the Buddha, the Dharma, and the Sangha. In its most outward explanation, this means that one believes in the truth of the Buddha's realization, the path or teachings that lead to this same realization, and the like-minded adepts who adopt these teachings and practices. Taking refuge may be founded purely on belief in the fundamental tenets of Buddhism, but ultimately, it should be a free act of will such as St. Augustine advised in regard to faith, or as Immanuel Kant might have put it, an act of pure intent. A more esoteric explanation of this Buddhist View might claim that the Buddha is in fact the pure and stable nature of one's intrinsic awareness (i.e. the Good), the Dharma the essence of one's thoughts and emotions, and the Sangha the very aggregates, winds and channels that form one's body and personality.

It is interesting to note that despite his deeply religious upbringing, Kant took refuge in the exercise of reason alone, for he claimed that only reason was autonomous. All acts not governed by this nimble faculty could be explained as compulsions, appetites and desires that, like all members of the animal kingdom, we are all obliged to obey—and obedience is not freedom, nor can simple submission to our animal appetites lead us to happiness. Despite this innate ability of reason to pilot our will beyond mere vegetative and animal responses, Kant also realized that reason is incapable of offering us any final answers or, at least, any truth-bearing claims that are beyond rational refutation. Such a request would be to ask more of reason than she is capable of giving. In his *Critique of Pure Reason* Kant demonstrated the very limits of reason itself, asserting that in the moral and aesthetic areas of human existence – realms of experience where we are forced to adopt conclusions about persons and matters as though these judgments were certain – pure reason could not provide conclusive judgments. This daunting task was left to what Kant referred to as practical reason (and what, as mentioned previously, Aristotle classified as *phronesis*). Although the peak of certainty could not be reached by reason alone, a kind of practical wisdom was still within reason's grasp.

Though we may be unaware of it, we all take refuge of one

sort or another in those verities of life we take to be irrefutable. For most of us, this simply consists in those views and dispositions we hold as truths by which to live. Everybody believes in something, if only for a reason to get up and dressed in the morning. We all must take refuge so that the doubt that stalks each one of us does not someday overtake and consume us. Our particular form of refuge may not be in the hidden Tao of Chuang Tzu, or the Three Jewels of Buddhism, in Allah as Creator, or even in the practical reason of Immanuel Kant, but it must be in something, even if it's only – as the iconic football coach Vince Lombardi once said – in "God, Family, and Football" (and not necessarily in that order). We are, in a word, compelled to anchor our minds and hearts in thoughts and feeling that provides us with a sense of physical, emotional and intellectual safety—whether we are Buddhists, Christians, scientists, or even devout atheists.

For many of us in contemporary times, our place of refuge exists both in the human intellect *and* in faith. I am referring, however, to that specific form of faith that provides an overall existential confidence – and includes the Sufi notion of sealing the heart. Paradoxically this faith rides on nothing in particular – i.e., as with the Great Way of Tao, no Unicorns are allowed; it grasps no particular object, requires no articles of belief to uphold or conceptual verities to justify. Faith of this sort embraces the fundamental intrigue and mystery of existence, all the while accepting the essentially unknowable nature of phenomena. Faith of this type also remains indifferent to Plantinga's PBB. We are speaking here of a faith not in God, Jesus, Muhammad, or Buddha, but faith that lies in the fundamentally pre-conceptual Truth of Reality. The late Buddhist adept and spiritual teacher Alan Watts (1915-1973) expressed it more simply as a trust in the process of letting go and being open to whatever the natural truth may eventually turn out to be. We should not, he advised, cling to an array of vested ideas and dogmatic assertions designed to support our faith. It's as though the enigma of Being precedes and actually produces all thoughts we might conjure about Reality. Thinking is always playing catch-up to

Truth. Thus faith could be described as the awareness within us of a metaphysical Truth that resides both within and beyond our human condition.

"One component of faith is a certain kind of affective psychological state—namely, a state of feeling confident and trusting.
Some philosophers hold that faith is to be identified simply with such a state: ... this may have been Wittgenstein's understanding. Faith in this sense—as one's overall 'default' attitude on life — provides a valuable foundation for flourishing: its loss is recognized as the psychic calamity of 'losing one's faith'." – *S.E.P.*

This does not mean that there is no Path to follow, no framework of virtue to live by, and no overarching purpose for which to strive – quite the contrary. Although the proof of one's particular faith does not rest on logical demonstration or irrefutable arguments, it does depend on the results – or as Aristotle might say, the flourishing – that faith produces in our character and in our conduct. Some would say there is no other measure of certain Truth. As Mahatma Gandhi advised: "Faith is not something to grasp, it is a state to grow into." Perhaps faith acts as a kind of seventh sense, an intuitive grasp of our inner nature that completes our understanding of what it means to be human.

EPILOGUE
THE MORAL OF THE STORY?

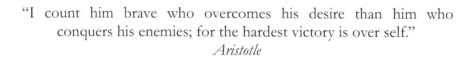

"I count him brave who overcomes his desire than him who conquers his enemies; for the hardest victory is over self."
Aristotle

FEINBERG'S EGOIST

"Imagine a person (let's call him 'Jones') who is, first of all, devoid of intellectual curiosity. He has no desire to acquire any kind of knowledge for its own sake, and thus is truly indifferent to questions of science, mathematics, and philosophy. Imagine further that the beauties of nature leave Jones cold: he is unimpressed by the autumn foliage, the snow-capped mountains, and the rolling oceans. Long walks in the country on spring mornings and skiing forays in the winter are to him equally a bore. Moreover, let us suppose that Jones can find no appeal in art. Novels are dull, poetry a pain, paintings nonsense, and music just noise.

"Suppose further that Jones has neither the participant's nor the spectator's passion for baseball, football, tennis, or any other sport. Swimming to him is a cruel aquatic form of calisthenics, the sun only a cause of sunburn. Dancing is coeducational idiocy, conversation a waste of time, the other sex an unappealing mystery. Politics is a fraud, religion mere superstition; and the misery of millions of underprivileged human beings is nothing to be concerned with or excited about. Suppose finally that Jones has no talent for any kind of handicraft, industry, or commerce, and that he does not regret that fact.

THE UNICORN PROBLEM

"What then is Jones interested in? He must desire something. To be sure, he does. Jones has an overwhelming passion for, a complete pre-occupation with, his own happiness. The one exclusive desire of his life is *to be happy*.

"Will Jones be able to satisfy his desire to be happy?"
Joel Feinberg (1926-2004)

THE ESSENCE OF UNICORNS

To live a life is to be forced into judgments, to draw conclusions about our daily experiences and to act accordingly. We are all compelled by this necessity in order to function at all. This is what I mean when I say we are all riding Unicorns whether we like it or not, since we must constantly cast our ballots, yea or nay, about problems that are in the most fundamental sense, unknowable. And when we do make our judgments regarding truth, knowledge, or even what determines "right action," we are in a sense making a bet on the essential quality of our lives, hoping that our reasoning or intuition provides the desired outcome or that we have acted from a positive intent. We make very few judgments – outside of pure logic, where definitions are absolute and the rules of order predetermined – that step completely outside the shadow of uncertainty. In fact, many if not most of our day-to-day judgments are wildly uncertain.

Although we can confidently claim to know that two plus two equals four, there are no propositions – especially moral propositions – that qualify as that about which we cannot possibly be wrong. Nonetheless, each one of us is obliged to justify in some manner the moral judgments we hold sacrosanct, and it is precisely here that the Unicorn Problem rears up to its full measure. There are numerous moral theories that attempt to explain or justify what human beings should or shouldn't do, what the right thing to do might be, or even what constitutes a moral principle in the first place, but none of them holds up absolutely in a real world situation. For example, Kant insisted that our moral duty was to always tell the truth – a consequence of his categorical imperative – but it seems reasonable enough for most of us to acknowledge that honesty is not always the best policy.

The problem here is: How do we each of us define what is moral, and how often do we review and reflect upon our own moral code? Despite the high likelihood that we exist in an amoral universe, existing as human beings demands moral judgments from us every day. Sam Harris, the neuroscientist, humanist and avid Rationalist, offers a wonderfully simple example of how reasoned thoughtfulness can lead us to appropriate moral judgments.

In one of his lectures he projects onto a large screen a picture of Muslim women heavily cloaked in their traditional burqas, covered from head to toe so that not even a sexually provocative ankle bone is exposed to prurient male eyes. Then he projects a second slide from the cover of one of the ubiquitous girlie magazines that fill the newsstands of our cities, young women wearing little to nothing, posed in purposefully provocative ways. He offers us two extreme views towards women specifically and human sexuality in general. He then asks: Doesn't reason (or call it common sense, for that matter) offer us a middle ground between these two extreme attitudes? Do we really require some higher moral authority, such as the Pope or an Imam, to guide us in such matters? Isn't practical reason sufficient when questioning the justifications of our moral decisions? Aren't our moral judgments, to a large extent, simply practical decisions that reasonable people are more than capable of making?

In addition, we might well wonder if our hunt for Truth and moral certitude actually arises from the very confusion and anxiety produced by a mind unsure of its own purpose and an overall human condition that feels anything but secure. Even though Aristotle reminds us that the desire to know and understand our lives is intrinsic to our very being, it may also be that Freud was not far from wrong when he defined humans as the 'neurotic animal'. Notwithstanding the dilemmas that moral issues present, perhaps our "Hero's Quest" for certain Truth is more a reflection of the human need for peace of mind rather than for moral prescriptions that promise personal happiness, be they based on reason or not. After all, as far back as the Hellenic period, the expressed goal of the inquiry into truth and knowledge was the attainment of tranquility, a mind at peace with itself. Many sages deemed the overcoming of subjective agitation to be the highest form of pleasure available to humankind... and the highest of human aspirations.

We might also wonder why we often have a sense of something missing in our lives, a pervasive sense of always needing something more – some elusive knowledge or missing element that is key to our personal happiness – that indefinable "thing" which we require in order to be truly at peace. Might this be a signal sent to us from the innermost depths of our being – an appeal from our most profound desire of all – what Nietzsche claimed is our inherent will to truth? Or is Santayana more to the point when he claims that the sixth sense of consciousness is itself a form of unease or strain, and therein lies the true ground of our dissatisfaction? Not to stray too far into a psychoanalytic labyrinth on this matter, we might also wonder if the sages, philosophers, and religious adepts from ancient times to the present day are correct in claiming that what all human beings desire above all else is happiness, what Socrates called the *Good*. Is achieving happiness the ultimate solution for a species that seems so plagued by anxiety, uncertainty, mistrust, false beliefs and unanswered prayers? If so, how do we achieve it? Let's not forget that, as Sandel points out in his lecture series on *Justice*, the spectators who witnessed Christians being eaten alive by lions in the Roman Coliseum seemed quite satisfied, even joyous, at the gruesome spectacle. Is this the type of spectacle that happiness would require of us? Or is it the case that happiness can only be the result of a soul at peace with itself? Might the *ataraxia* of the ancient Skeptics, the *apathia* of the Stoics, or even the *non-attachment* of Buddhists, be both the intent and the goal of the examined life that Socrates claimed was the sole redeeming factor of our short lives here on earth?

In the final analysis, we find that any cherished convictions we might cling to regarding absolute truth kicks up yet another Unicorn, that ubiquitous, figurative embodiment of our need for certainty. If this is so, then another view we might consider is that our thirst for certainty – for the actual reasons and insights that stand behind all phenomena, our need for happiness included – is merely an intellectual puzzle with no final solution, and therefore a waste of the precious little time that is afforded each human life. It might very well be reasonable to conclude that our desire for certainty could be founded on psychological needs alone, ultimately reflecting our emotional immaturity and inherent insecurity as a species, and an aspect of what is today termed evolutionary epistemology. Perhaps we are finally forced to the conclusion that happiness truly is the final goal of our epistemological journeys and that this ultimate goal is achievable, according to Aristotle, through the cultivation of a magnanimity of spirit and the actualization of our intellectual and moral potential. Perhaps he was on to something profound in claiming, "Happiness is the meaning and the purpose of life, the whole aim and end of human existence."

Most of us realize however, that true happiness is not a static condition: The questions, doubts, confusion and uncertainties that our everyday experiences visit on us appear unavoidable, and any permanent state of joy or good cheer remains elusive at best. Beyond this, most of us are intuitively aware of how we have failed to actualize (to use Aristotle's term) our own potential. And while there are no infallible ways to eliminate doubt from our lives, we are nonetheless capable of integrating our minds and hearts – our reason and our faith – in the hope that we too are embraced by a magnanimity of spirit, and consoled by a soul at peace with itself.

As the fourteenth Dalai Lama (1935 -) put it: "Inner peace is the key: If you have inner peace, the external problems do not affect your deep sense of peace and tranquility…without this inner peace, no matter how comfortable your life is materially, you may still be worried, disturbed, or unhappy because of circumstances."

***

THE UNICORN PROBLEM

Despite tens of thousands of years on this earth, humankind has found no final answers to the recurring problems of each generation, no irrefutable solutions to such perennial questions as What is Truth? What is Mind? What is Reality? What is Good? and finally, What is Happiness? If we were asked to define what makes for happiness in our lives, would it be beyond words, in the same way that the definition of a "soul at peace" implies? It seems that this last question, What is Happiness? proves to be the most difficult and intriguing question of all.

How do we reconcile our selfish interest in being happy with our moral responsibility to others? Are we our 'brother's keeper' or do we have an innate conflict with that moral duty? In the last analysis, it might surprise us to consider how often we use the word "happy" to express how we feel throughout the day; i.e., we are "happy" to see a friend; "happy" about our kids' performance in school; "happy" that the sun is shining today; "happy" with a recent purchase; the salesperson is "happy to help", etc. These fleeting moments are naturally a part of the normal person's day, but we also know they are only temporary states of mind and not what we ultimately mean when we say, like Jones in Feinberg's thought-experiment, that we seek true happiness in this life. The Buddhist saint Nagarjuna sums up the human dilemma this way: "After happiness comes suffering. After suffering arises happiness. For beings happiness and suffering revolve like a wheel."

In reprising Jones's dilemma...what should we believe? Will he find the happiness that he desires more than all else? Is he on the right track, showing us the kind of radical renunciation required of all human beings in order to be happy? Is this the ascetic ideal taken to its logical conclusion? Or should we take Aristotle's view when he states: "To avoid criticism say nothing, do nothing, be nothing?"

Perhaps Jones is practicing the kind of selfishness that blurs into solipsism? One of my students responded to this thought experiment by writing: "...he will be destined to only achieve frustration while figuratively chasing his own tail, caught in a paradox. Those who are happy achieve such a state by the pursuit of activities or interests that fulfill a Separate desire (or a set of Separate desires) outside of happiness, which Jones does not have if he literally has a 'complete preoccupation with' his own happiness."

Feinberg's thought experiment is a refutation (critique) of the moral philosophy referred to as psychological egoism. This moral view states that all of our acts, including those acts most might call altruistic or even heroic, are solely motivated by a desire for personal well-being. This is the moral perspective proffered by Plato's brother Glaucan, who argued that we are all egoists by nature and that our self-interest alone is paramount. The novelist Ayn Rand (1905-1982) took this view one step further, insisting that not only are we egoists by nature, but that we *should* be morally selfish; we have no moral obligations to be our "brother's keeper." Each of us must be primarily concerned with our own well-being; it's just a fact of what it means to be human.

In his thought experiment Feinberg is essentially asking us: if all our concerns for anything other than the express desire for our own personal happiness were eliminated, would we then be happy? Would happiness come to us as a kind of default condition, the reward for (or the consequence of) abandoning any interest in social affairs or in the fate of others? It seems not, and we could predict with a fair amount of certainty that poor Jones' hedonistic desire for his personal happiness – his obsessive focus on living without concern for the welfare of others – actually would be counter to his self-interests. Hence it appears that psychological egoism is but another Unicorn disguised as some kind of self-evident, morally rewarding workhorse.

"Two things will seemingly hold: (a) such a person would eventually lack friends, close relationships, etc. *and* (b) this will lead to much unhappiness. This seems problematic for a theory that says all of our ultimate desires are for our own wellbeing." – *S.E.P.*

The second problem with the strictly egoist perspective is that it is self-validating: the proof given for egoism is to say that any and all moral acts are done purely out of self-interest. The claim and the premise that substantiates the claim are one and the same, and the

THE UNICORN PROBLEM

overall argument is therefore yet another circular argument. This is analogous to saying that God exists because it says so in the Bible—and the Bible is the word of God. If it's impossible for moral actions to be governed by anything other than self-interest, then how do we test this truth-bearing claim? We find that it is not falsifiable.

> "... at this point we may suspect that they are holding their theory in a "privileged position" – that of immunity to evidence, that they would allow no *conceivable* behavior to count as evidence against it." – *S.E.P.*

And what does it mean to act only out of self-interest, such that every moral sentiment collapses onto a private island? Is this the same as selfishness or is this simply the egocentric predicament as described by psychologists and philosophers, now recast as a moral principle?

The Tulku Gyaltrul Rimpoche (1925 -), a venerated teacher from the Nyingmapa tradition of Vajrayana Buddhism, explained the Buddhist concept of "ego" by telling a story. He briefly recounted his escape from Tibet into India, and how, on more than one occasion his group was ambushed and fired upon by Communist soldiers and assorted bandits. When the bullets flew, he said, everyone ducked—including himself. This impulse towards self-preservation was his example of how thoroughly the egocentric predicament permeates our nature. As a consequence, he realized the profound difficulty it would entail to move beyond this human condition in which we all find ourselves. All too often, it is the basic necessities and exigencies of life that keep us preoccupied with our own welfare and self-serving interests and impede our progress towards what we desire most: personal happiness. And for Buddhists, personal happiness is only possible through liberation from all illusion, including the illusion of ego.

We might also wonder if it is even possible to know the meaning of *self-interest* or *selfishness* if we have no altruistic acts with which to compare it? Isn't this a failure to recognize the suppressed correlative in the very term "selfish?"

"...Until we know what they [psychological egoists] would count as *unselfish* behavior, we can't very well know what they mean when they say that all voluntary behavior is *selfish*." – S.E.P.

It could be that Feinberg's egoist ultimately intuited that our worldly desires are the final impediment to personal peace of mind and happiness. This approach is reminiscent of the ascetic path proposed by religious traditions, both East and West. In the Christian tradition for instance, we are told that during his 40-day-fasting retreat in the Judean desert, Jesus was tempted by Satan, who appeared to him with offers of extravagant worldly powers and untold riches, on the condition that Jesus bowed to him as his Ruler (I think we have a pretty good idea how that conversation went). As a consequence the early Church Fathers also strove to set aside all worldly desires – much as does Feinberg's egoist – their hearts set on one goal alone: union with God. In a like fashion, Hindu and Buddhist doctrine claims that our attachment to mundane affairs, the desires and hopes that fill our daily lives, as well as our fears of loss, is what separates us from our innate Buddha nature. It is said that the Buddha rejected the temptations of Mara – worldly ambitions and desires – and was finally liberated from cyclic existence.

In the ancient Taoist tradition Chuang Tzu speaks of the "fasting of the heart": "...There is then a direct grasp of what is right there before you that can never be heard with the ear or understood with the mind. Fasting of the heart empties the faculties, frees you from limitation and from preoccupation. Fasting of the heart begets unity and freedom."

There is one critical difference between these accounts of renunciation and Feinberg's egoist, however: the egoist still remains trapped in a cage of his own making, wrought by his one profound desire for happiness, unaware that only he holds the key.

***

THE UNICORN PROBLEM

After all is said and done, the true Path to a fulfilled life as modeled by Socrates cannot be found in the many scholarly books on the subject or even in the sophisticated arguments of philosophers, but rather it is found in the deliberate and intentional contemplation of the human condition, and more importantly, in the enactment of the significant moral principles and ethical standards by which we choose to live our lives. If Feinberg's hapless Jones were to actually find the happiness he sought, I believe he would have to first take a long detour through a thoroughly examined life. We have already considered how attachment to our opinions, beliefs, and convictions, including our belief in true and certain facts, can lead us astray, transferring us from one impassable boundary to another, those very places where Unicorns abound. If the good life, the flourishing life, the happy life is indeed our final goal, then maybe Socrates was correct when he counseled that the unexamined life is not worth living. Or maybe I'm grossly overstating the problem, and the whole process is much simpler than we suppose. Perhaps Feinberg's egoist should follow the additional counsel of Socrates when he said: "My advice to you is to get married: if you find a good wife, you'll be happy. If not, you'll become a philosopher."

Some of us have been fortunate enough to do both.

AFTERWORD

"Thinking is the soul talking to itself."
Plato

It is my ardent wish that this book be of benefit to all those seekers of truth who prize self-honesty above all virtues, especially in addressing the motivations of their actions. In this way it is directed towards self-reflective souls who walk in the footsteps of Thales, Shakyamuni Gautama, Socrates, Hypatia, St. Aquinas, St. Anselm, Rene Descartes, Sir Isaac Newton, Bishop Berkeley, David Hume, Immanuel Kant, Albert Einstein, Bertrand Russell, Gandhi, Elizabeth Anscombe, Anna Arendt, Eric Fromm, The Dalai Lama, Thomas Merton, Hilary Putnam, Sessela Bok…the real heroes of the examined life.

I leave the reader with these final words from Bertrand Russell from his book, *Problems of Philosophy*: "The world of being is unchangeable, rigid, exact, delightful to the mathematician, the logician, the builder of metaphysical systems, and all who love perfection more than life. The world of existence is fleeting, vague, without sharp boundaries, without any clear plan or arrangement, but it contains all thoughts and feelings, all the data of sense, and all physical objects, everything that can do either good or harm, everything that makes any difference to the value of life and the world. According to our temperaments, we shall prefer the contemplation of the one or of the other."

ACKNOWLEDGMENTS

Despite the pure joy of the creative enterprise and those rare moments when one actually writes down what one means to say, writing a book and bringing it to completion is difficult. I could not have done it without help. At the top of the list of those to thank is my wife, Deidre, whose ongoing encouragement, support and editing skills made me think that maybe I could achieve my goal. Also, my primary editor Julie Akins, whose suggestions helped clarify confusing passages and eliminate sections that did not promote the overall theme of the book. I am indebted to my friend and colleague Prakash Chenjeri. His insistence on conceptual clarity compelled me to rethink and rewrite more than one chapter. Sarah Rose Marshank read one of the earliest, comparatively rough versions of this book, and her smile of approval and helpful hints let me know that a final version was worth pursuing. Finally, I thank my mother, Sherana Harriette Frances, for her patient and generous proofreading of the countless earlier versions of the manuscript and for her unflagging and "unbiased" enthusiasm for this book.

Made in the USA
San Bernardino, CA
25 March 2017